FAMOUS FIGURES OF
CHRIST COLLEGE
BRECON

By

Jonathan Morgan

ABOUT THE AUTHOR

Jonathan Morgan was educated at Christ College, Brecon, R.M.A. Sandhurst, and Aberystwyth, Cardiff and Glamorgan Universities. He also taught at U.W.I.C. (now Cardiff Metropolitan) for nine years. Jonathan's father, the Rev. G Rex Morgan, Chaplain to the King's Royal Rifle Corps and Senior Housemaster at Christ College, Brecon, was a well-known prisoner-of-war and was on the dreadful 'Shoe Leather Express' March in Poland. It is interesting that Christ College former pupils won 23 MCs in the First World War.

Jonathan's was a great Welsh sporting family which included Guy Morgan, Captain of Cambridge University and Wales at rugby and Glamorgan at Cricket, and Dr. Teddy Morgan, Captain of Wales and the British Lions at rugby. Rex's cousin Guy (not the rugby player), was a Royal Navy Lieutenant and prisoner-of-war who wrote the well-known play 'Albert R.N.'. Jonathan's mother, Glenys, was the daughter of Captain T.L.Morgan, Adjutant of the 15th Welsh in the early part of the Great War.

As well as a sportsman himself, Jonathan is a 3rd Order Anglican Franciscan. He was invalided out of the Army with PTSD or related illness in 1980 and had served with the Royal Regiment of Wales as a Captain which included an horrific tour of Northern Ireland in the Ardoyne and Bone district of Belfast.

ABOUT THE ILLUSTRATOR

Robert Macdonald, an artist who lives near Brecon, is a past Chair of the Welsh Group, the senior association of professional artists in Wales, and President of the Royal Watercolour Society of Wales. He is a graduate of the Royal College of Art. Born in 1935, his childhood was shaped by the upheavals of the Second World War. After losing their home in a wartime bombing raid the Macdonalds emigrated to New Zealand in 1945. Robert did military service in the New Zealand Army.

He returned to Britain in 1958 and studied at the London Central School of Art. Since coming to live in Wales with his Welsh-born wife Annie he has been inspired by the Welsh landscape and mythology.

CONTENTS

FOREWORD

I started as a day pupil at Christ College in September 1949. I still have a vivid recollection of my first day in the School. My first lesson in the Lower School, as it was called, was a veritable culture shock for a young lad from a country primary school - Latin. The whole class was made to recite aloud together the declension of *mensa* by rote. The first declension of the Latin noun has been deeply embedded in my subconscious from that day forward. The Latin master was G Rex Morgan. Later that day a second unforgettable experience - my first game of rugby football. As a small boy of ten I was put on the wing in an under thirteens game. The referee and coach was G Rex Morgan. In those days Rex, as one of the few 'young' members of staff, was everywhere. He coached rugby and cricket (at all levels), was housemaster of the Hostel (later renamed Donaldsons after A E Donaldson, its housemaster for many years) and taught all manner of subjects to junior forms. Later he became Chaplain and in that capacity was a huge influence on me as well as being a very dear friend.

Jonathan is, as he tells us here, the first-born of Rex and Glenys, his wife, born when they were houseparents of the Hostel, which was Jonathan's home for the first thirteen years of his life. You could say with categorical certainty therefore that Christ College is a basic element in Jonathan's DNA. Christ College is in his blood. The School is one of his first and abiding loves, a love which is manifestly evident in the pages of this book.

The book consists of a miscellany of historical narrative and idiosyncratic reminiscence about a variety of different individuals associated with Christ College, who have distinguished themselves one way or another in a particular

1

field of endeavour. It is, in essence, a personal selection; it makes no claim to be a comprehensive historical account.

We start with the origins of the foundation and of the School, so there are introductory chapters on the Dominican Friary founded on the site and on Henry VIII, the School's founder. Jonathan then highlights the contribution of Breconians to the Church, the military, to culture, including the visual arts, to the legal profession, to politics and to sport, predominantly rugby football. Alongside these chapters there are more personal reminiscences on families. Including Jonathan's own, on his father, Rex Morgan, (a moving act of *pietas*), and on Jonathan himself. The only female highlighted in this otherwise exclusively male story is represented in the personal account of her unique experience by Tori James, the first Welsh woman to climb Everest.

All this is presented with sensitivity and affection. Jonathan's pride in the achievements of Christ College is evident on every page. Others would no doubt make a different selection of distinguished individual Breconians, but what Jonathan has assembled here will be of enormous interest to *alumni* of Christ College and friends of the School everywhere. Like me, they will certainly learn new things about that unique institution, Christ College, Brecon.

D P Davies

INTRODUCTION

The author was made very much aware of the pecking order of the public school system when he went to a smart English prep school in Devon from Wales. Christ College Brecon seemed to be quite low on this order.

This was the start for the author, of an inferiority complex, as Christ College was his destination after prep school. On doing research for this book, he realised that there was no need for such thoughts as it is truly a school of great depth and antiquity.

In this book, he explores many notables who went to the school; its early foundation by a Tudor and its prominence as one of the few great public schools of Wales, a country not possessing many of these. Like all authors, he has a slant on the school towards sport and the military. His nine relatives that were there were all involved in sport, some at the highest level and it is probable that no other rugby family in Wales has as many first class players. Also, there is a chapter on his father who has always been very understated but was a highly brave man under circumstances way and beyond sport, and who served the school with great popularity. The school, after being for so many years single sex has become coeducational, marketing itself now as an International Welsh School with a sister school in Malaysia.

It has not been possible to mention all who have given tremendous support to this school and there is a bias towards the author's own time there as a young boy growing up and as a pupil. It was always a no-nonsense sort of school, without a lot of snobbery, which enabled its pupils to mix in most company outside and to present themselves favourably.

The author thanks Professor D P Davies for his stewardship of the school as chairman of governors and also the bishops who were chairmen, Dr John Sharp and Mr Michael Jepson for steering the school through times that sometimes proved difficult. It has survived. It still maintains its Welsh flavour, but now has a big International input, especially from the Far East. It has been known for its sport, its music and its scholarship and still thrives. The present chair of governors is Sir Paul Silk, who was a great friend of the authors when he was a boy there and put three sons through the school.

Thank you so much to Huw Richards for all he does for the Old Breconians and the information he has given me for this book.

Acknowledgements

Frances Chaffey for her secretarial services.
Huw Richards for his great help.
Alison Crocket for proof reading.

THE DOMINICANS

THE DOMINICANS AT THE BRECON FRIARY

The Dominican order is also known as The Order of Preachers and is a mendicant Catholic religious order founded by the Spanish priest Dominic of Caleruega in France and approved by Pope Honorius III via the Papal Bull 'Religiosam Vitam' on 22 December 1216. Dominic founded the order to preach the gospel and to oppose heresy. The teaching activity of the order and its scholastic organisation placed the preachers in the forefront of the intellectual life of the Middle Ages.

Dominic became a canon at the cathedral of Osma in 1195 and in 1205 he started preaching against the Catholics of the Languedoc. Goaded by his lack of success he hit on the idea of using schools to teach the Catholic faith, one of the many ideas he poached from the Cathars. From a secular point of view, there was no harm at all in the Cathars and no reason for them to be even mildly persecuted, let alone burnt alive. Modern Dominicans consistently deny that Dominic ever exercised the office of inquisitor, pointing out that the Papal Inquisition was formally constituted only after Dominic's death. There is no doubt that the Dominicans spawned the medieval Inquisition with all its horrors, pioneering new methods of torture and itemising new crimes. Dominic died at the age of 51, having reached the Convent of St Nicholas at Bologna, Italy, exhausted by the labours and austerities of his career.

It is interesting that the patron saint of the Friary of Brecon is St Nicholas as he is also the patron saint of Greece and particularly the Hellenic Navy. It is probably because of Dominic's association with and his death at the Convent of St Nicholas that the Brecon Friary has him as its patron saint.

There is no record of the date of the foundation of Brecon Friary or the name of its founder, but it could not have been in existence earlier than AD 1221. It was built on the ground that lay adjacent to the ford over the river Usk to Brecon, helping to safeguard this crossing. The mission of the friars was to travel about the country preaching the truths of Christianity. They professed the strictest rule of poverty, and from their dress, which consisted of a black cloak with a hood worn over a white woollen robe, they were known as Black Friars. As for its founder, it was probably one or other of the Plantagenets, although the local family, The Awbreys, might have had a hand in it. It boasted the distinction of being the largest Dominican friary in Wales.

The Spanish Queen of England, Eleanor of Castille was keen on the friars' work, for under her will in 1291 the Priory of Brecon received a legacy of 100 shillings, a large sum for those days. In 1335, the Prior was deposed and there is some folklore that one of the friars was murdered, which might have occurred at this time. This later gave rise to a rumour according to which the ghost of Bishop Lucy haunted the chapel, but in truth, it was probably the ghost of the murdered friar who was buried there.

The chapel, as we see it now, is only part of what was a much larger building and under what is now the nave, the remains of a number of the Gam family were buried. Dafydd Gam was a captain in the King's Archers at Agincourt, but there is no evidence, according to the Garter King of Arms, that he was knighted there. On August 29 1538, there was a voluntary surrender by the Prior Richard David and nine friars, into the hands of the suffragen Bishop of Dover acting for the King, Henry VIII; the surrender document in the public record office shows the signatures of the friars. Two at least were illiterate and made their mark only. According to the Bishop, 'The friary is well builded, hath no lead, hath certain meadows and orchards and no chalise or jewel'. Lands amounting to six and a half acres or more were let to Llewelyn ap Morgan. No damage seems to have been done to the buildings at this time.

References:
'Christ College Brecon 1541-1991, An Illustrated History' by E G Parry (published on the occasion of the school's 450th anniversary 1991, Wales)

HENRY VIII

HENRY VIII

In 1485, Henry Tudor defeated Richard III at the Battle of Bosworth. Henry was a Welshman, and the involvement of Welsh soldiers at Bosworth played a significant part in Henry's victory. After he became king, Henry rewarded many Welshmen with government posts in London. In 1509, Henry VIII succeeded his father to the throne. Henry did not have the same feel for Wales as his father had, although he still maintained the Welsh dragon on his heraldic insignia. Henry VIII was very concerned with the way the marcher lords, who ran much of the border country, governed their lands. In particular, he thought many criminals were committing offences in England and then escaping across the Welsh border. It was reported that one marcher lord received payment from twenty-three murderers and twenty-five robbers in return for being protected from English justice.

Also, after the split from the Roman Catholic Church, Henry questioned the loyalty of many marcher lords who were Roman Catholic. So, he decided to take full control of Wales and remove their power. Between 1536 and 1543 a series of laws were passed in Parliament which became known as the Act of Union. The marcher lands disappeared and the whole of Wales was divided into shires or counties and each one had a justice of the peace. Wales was represented in Parliament, although Welsh was not spoken there, and the law courts in Wales conducted their affairs in English only. If you wanted to make your way in London, or socially, as a young Welshman, you had to speak English. One of the bonuses of the new legislation, however, was the abolition of many of the restrictions imposed upon the Welsh after the Glyndwr revolt against the English which began in 1400 and lasted for five years.

Before the dissolution of the monasteries, Bishop Rawlins of St Davids made application to the King for a transfer to Brecon. He portrayed the inhabitants of the town at that time as 'a parcel of illiterate and beggarly savages, ignorant alike of their duty to God and man' who were sadly in need of the influence of a prebendal body. Bishop Barlow, who succeeded Rawlins, also made scathing remarks about 'the barefoot rascals of Brecon'.

In 1541 a scheme was put forward by Bishop Barlow of St David's that the college of Abergwilli, Carmarthenshire be removed to Brecon and established on the lands and in the buildings of the Friary of St Nicholas.

Henry VIII agreed to Rawlins moving to Brecon so that the new college could improve the morals and amend the manners of the King's liege subjects in the vicinity. Rawlins thus became a founder of Christ College. The school was endowed with an annual income of £53 and became a grammar school with 3 masters, the learned grammar master, the divinity instructor and an usher as its teaching staff. Free education was offered to all those who wished to receive it, and an annual sum of £24 was specially set apart for the maintenance of 20 poor scholars. In 1547, the charity commissioners inspected and reported favourably on the school. There was also an elementary department teaching the alphabet to very young children. The old connection with the friary was continued, as on each December 6th, St Nicholas Night, the scholars held a feast when the sexton rang the church bell to summon them to the hostel, where each boy spent 3 pence for cakes and ale.

The armorial bearings and the motto of the school were not created and finalised until 1976. The shield consists of a cross containing the letter 'H' surmounted by a crown for King Henry VIII and the cross of Bishop William Barlow whose lion serves as part of the crest. The tower refers to Eleanor of Castille, the earliest known benefactor of the Friary of St Nicholas. The lion has been crowned as a reference to a Royal Visitor to the college and holds a pipe which is part of Bishop Lucy's arms.

As well as being one of the college's prominent benefactors, Bishop Lucy has given the school its ghost and legend.

11

The armorial bearing of the school depicts a lion, having about his shoulders the red mantle adopted from the arms and mayoralty of the town from whence the school draws a significant number of its pupils. The crest wreath runs around the helm in white and green representing the Tudor livery colours. The green and gold of the mantling represent the Royal Foundation and are still used today as the 1st XV colours. The school motto of 'Possunt Quia Posse Videntur' translated means 'They achieve because they believe they can'. The history of this school is extremely significant, as being founded by the Tudors, the boys tended not to be affected by an inferiority complex because the Tudors, with their largely Welsh army, beat a larger English army. That was the last time the two nations fought each other. And although Henry VIII was a terrible man, the Tudors have left a lasting impression on British history.

JOHN PENRY

13

LINKS WITH JESUS COLLEGE OXFORD

JOHN PENRY THE MARTYR AND TWO FAMOUS PREBENDARIES

There have always been close links between Christ College Brecon and Jesus College Oxford. Jesus was founded by Hugh Price who was a Welsh lawyer and clergyman, born in Brecon, the son of a butcher. In 1571, Price petitioned Elizabeth I to formally establish Jesus College Oxford. She was keen to have a Welsh Protestant college at Oxford and he provided a lot of the funds, although one or two of the mortgages he took out were fairly suspect. The Queen claimed the title of founder of the college and although Dr Price was too old to have attended Christ College, Brecon, because of his dates and those of its foundation, there was always a close connection. However, according to the archivist at Jesus College, he cannot find any references to closed scholarships.

During January 1666-67, one Rice Powell of Boughrood, Radnor, handed over some land to trustees of Jesus College to be sold for various purposes. One of them was that £25 a year should be given to the principal and fellows of Jesus College, Oxford to support '2 poor schollars' there who should be 'natives of the counties of Radnor and Brecon or one of them the relation and kindred of the said Rice Powell.' So he explicitly endowed scholarships at Jesus College to support promising lads from Brecon and Radnor. From what the archivist could deduce of the significance of the College, he would imagine that for a lad in this age, going to the College would be the best, if not the only way, he would get the education for him to apply for and get the scholarship for higher education. Also, for many years the author believes, one of the governors of Christ College was a representative of Jesus College as well.

John Penry was born and bred in a farmhouse called Cefn Brith which stands on the north side of Mynydd Epynt in Breconshire, not far from Llangammarch. He was born in 1553, five years after the accession of Queen Elizabeth I to the throne of England and went to Christ College, Brecon where he learned Latin and Greek grammar and would practise Latin conversation with his teacher and his fellow pupils. He was taught English, and in the scripture lessons he learned the Ten Commandments, the Lord's Prayer and the Apostolic Creed. When he was 17, he went to Cambridge where he spent four years at Peterhouse, graduating in 1584 with a BA degree. After that he proceeded to Merton College, Oxford, where he earned an MA.

Meanwhile, he had formed links with friends in Northampton, many of whom were Puritans and when he returned to Breconshire in 1587 he wrote a book, begging Her Majesty and Parliament to institute measures that would be effective in bringing the Gospel to Wales. He requested that laymen in Wales should be permitted to preach and asked for voluntary contributions from the people for the maintenance of a greater number of preachers. However, his book was construed by Whitgift, the Archbishop of Canterbury, as an attack on the clergy, and Henry was ordered to retract certain statements, which he refused to do. A large number of Penry's first books were destroyed by order of the High Commission but despite spending some time in prison, Penry brought out another book called 'The Exaltation'. In this book we find again a strong plea for the Gospel in Welsh. In his first book 'Aequity', Penry had pleaded to have the complete Bible in Welsh. He now rejoiced to understand that William Morgan's translation was ready for printing. Penry had engaged the services of a secret press run by someone called Waldergrave which was eventually hidden in Fawsley House, Northampton shire, which belonged to Sir Richard Knightly.

If we read the tracts that were printed while Penry and his

secret press were fleeing from one hiding place to another, we find that their author was again writing of the pitiful conditions of his beloved country. After this, Penry, because of persecution by Bishop Whitgift and his court, went up to Scotland for three years. When Queen Elizabeth heard of this she was furious with James, King of Scotland for granting refuge to a fugitive from Wales. James was, in consequence, obliged to call Penry an outlaw. Penry said, 'It hath been my purpose always to employ my small talent in my small country of Wales where I know that the poor people perish for want of knowledge.' One author said of him, 'His heart was still in Wales.'

He returned, not to Wales, but to London. Then on 22nd March 1593 he was taken prisoner and remained in the prison Poultly Compter where he carried on protesting against his unjust treatment. He wrote to Lord Burghley without success; his wife petitioned the Queen but she herself was thrown in prison. Penry was perceived as being part of the Separatists, people who refused to worship according to the Established Church. He came up in front of the King's Bench and the Lord Chief Justice Popham and was indicted on two counts: first, that of inciting the country to sedition and to rebellion against the Queen and second, for treason, in that he opposed the Queen as head of the Established Church. He wrote again to Lord Burghley after this saying, 'I am a poor young man born and bred in the mountains of Wales. I am the first since the last springing up of the Gospel in this latter age that publicly laboured to have the Blessed Seed thereof sown in these barren mountains.'

Penry did appear before Lord Burghley, insisting that he was utterly innocent of the charges brought against him. Then on Tuesday 29th May 1593 he was told he was to be put to death. He was dragged on a hurdle through the narrow streets of the city of London to St Thomas a Watering where he was hanged in the open air. But none of his friends or family were present and no one knows where he was buried. His bravery and his complete dedication to the cause of Christ remain an inspiration in Wales to this day. Undoubtedly, he was one of the greatest sons of Christ College, Brecon.

The prebendal system which had been brought from Abergwilli consisted of twenty-three stalls. Three of these stalls were held by the Decanuscancallar Precentor. The names of the others vary at different dates and few of the prebendaries resided either continually or occasionally at the College. The prebendaries gave certain of their prebends or ancient pensions towards the lecturers and school. One of them was Sir Philip Sidney whose father was Sir Henry Sidney, Lord President of the Marches. He held the prebend of Llangwinllo, Radnorshire. He was a writer of some note, a diplomat and a militant Protestant. In 1586, he joined Sir John Norris in the Battle of Zutphen, fighting for the Protestant cause against the Spanish. During the battle, he was shot in the thigh and died of gangrene twenty-six days later at the age of 31. As he lay dying, Sidney composed a song to be sung on his deathbed. According to the story, while lying wounded he gave his water to another wounded soldier saying,' Thy necessity is greater than mine.' His figure was one of great romance, and it is marvellous that his name is associated with Christ College, Brecon.

Another famous, or infamous, prebendary of Christ College was William Dodd 1729-1777. He was an English Anglican clergyman and a man of letters who lived extravagantly and was nicknamed, 'The Macaroni Parson'. He dabbled in forgery in an effort to clear his debts, was caught, convicted and despite a public campaign for a Royal pardon, was hanged at Tyburn for forgery.

The early 19th century was a real dark age for the school. The prebendal system fell into hopeless corruption. In days notorious for absenteeism and misuse of ancient endowments, the headmaster and prebends were mostly absentees or pluralists and the buildings were, in the main, too ruinous for use. But in 1851, the Christ College Act of Parliament got rid of the old body of prebendaries and a modern public school with a board of governors was established in its place.

ARCHBISHOP GLYN SIMON

PRIESTS AND PRELATES

It is no wonder that Christ College has produced so many distinguished priests, who were influenced by the holiness of the remains of the Dominican Friary chapel. Bishop Lucy, who was involved in the school in the late 17th century, is described on his monument as 'a shining star in the Anglican Church'. Among dissenters, he is remembered as a vengeful persecutor and we have already discussed the story of his ghost. George Bull, educated at Blundells, where the author taught for twelve years was another popular bishop at the time, who took an interest in Christ College, as well as being a theologian of European renown.

Another man whose 150th anniversary we celebrated in 1964 was Thomas Coke who was born in 1747. When he matured he was only five feet one inch tall and had a tendency to put on weight, but he was a live wire who started off as an Anglican but after meeting John Wesley in August 1776, turned his back on the Church of England.

The year 1784 was a momentous one both for Methodism and for Thomas Coke, the young man from Christ College who had studied jurisprudence at Jesus College Oxford. The year also saw the culmination of his service as Wesley's administrative assistant in the drafting of the Deed of Declaration which gave legal status to the Methodist Conference and ensured the continuance of Methodism after its founder's death. Coke engaged in a bewildering number and variety of activities, continuing to be involved in the affairs of the British connection but at the same time he was superintendent of the world mission of the Church, to which he was devoted, and a bishop of the Methodist Episcopal Church of America. After a huge amount of work with Methodism, especially associated with the mission in America, he eventually died on a sea trip in May 1814. He was a great man.

Another great man, who was a notable pupil and achieved eminence under the headmastership of David Griffith in the late 1890s was Thomas Price, who came to be known as *Carnhuanawc*. His work was known throughout Europe for its untiring enthusiasm for Wales, its language and its people. It was also a central part of his vision to place the Welsh nation in a European context. But however wide his horizons must have been, he lived and worked in Breconshire, the county of his birth. He was generations ahead of his time in his example of how to foster patriotism and in his love for mankind in general, and love of the common people. Indeed, he lived through turbulent times, with the strains of the long Napoleonic Wars and the early days of the Industrial Revolution.

Nearer to home, Wales was seething with social discontent with the activities of the Rebecca Riots in west Wales, the 1832 Merthyr Rising, and the Scotch Cattle activists in south east Wales. At school in Christ College Price was quite an attentive pupil, interested in stars, mechanics, geometry and the world of nature. A natural craftsman, he enjoyed wood carving and also amused himself making drawings of his friends.

During his time at Christ College, French prisoners of war were billeted in the town and local tradition tells of them taking their afternoon stroll along Captain's Walk. The late Professor Thomas J Williams argued that the French officers were mainly Bretons, who spoke Breton and fired Thomas Price's enthusiasm for the Breton language and for Brittany. The translation of the Bible into Breton became a lifelong crusade. The officers and the young student also shared more conventional gentlemanly interests, and time was found to improve both their swordsmanship and their mathematics.

Price was one of the Kerry Group of churchmen determined to make the Church of England more welcoming to Welsh speakers. One way was to encourage eisteddfodau in each of the Church's four provinces in Wales. He believed in the eisteddfod as an institution that inspired a national spirit and the love of country. A handsome and conspicuously noble- looking man, he was said to have looked young when middle aged. He was a kind, courteous, modestly mannered man who dressed in clothes made of homespun materials, as did his parishioners. Although he loved country life, he detested blood sports and shooting, preferring rowing and fishing. He was very much involved with Lady Llanover and the great revival of Welsh patriotism. Her society contacts increased the status and prestige of the cultural movements to raise the prominence of the Welsh language. Thomas Price was a giant of his time.

Another more recent prelate was Glyn Simon. The school house in which Glyn lived in Christ College until he became a day boy in 1915 was, in his view, a wilderness, where not even a mouse would have been able to be quiet and safe. However, for the headmaster, Robert Haley Chambers, he had great admiration. He gave Glyn true classical teaching at its best. But the key figure on the staff at that time was Canon A E Donaldson who was a man who spent much of his life as a housemaster at Christ College and had a huge influence on the pupils. He also protected and built up the archives, although these really only go back to the 1880s. He succeeded in conveying to Glyn, when he was preparing him for confirmation, that this was an event in one's life which was of the greatest importance. He also brought out the essential moral strength and teaching of the catechism. Donaldson was a sincere Christian whose convictions broke through the reserve which too often hampers us when we deal with things of the spirit.

Glyn Simon summed up his time in Brecon by saying, 'Although I had some happy experiences, the price I paid was too high. My confidence in myself disappeared, in so far as it existed at the time, being replaced with a considerable shyness, suspicion and distrust of my fellow men. On the good side I would put the indefinable influence of beautiful architecture and the long history that accompanied it. I was given a classical education by a fine classical scholar, introduced to good English and a sound grounding in grammar and syntax. On the bad side,

I was introduced at the age of ten to an entirely new way of life. In many ways it was brutish and crude, bullying was rife and the average standard of intelligence not very good. But the general bullying and unpopularity which was my lot left me permanently unsure of myself, shy and awkward with strangers, especially loud voiced and fluent, self-confident people.'

During the early years, Glyn was engaged in training young clergymen at the hostel in Bangor. Among the freshmen who presented themselves at the hostel in 1932 was R S Thomas, who himself admits that he was gauche and without the taste for learning. His first impressions of the warden were of 'a slight, red-cheeked, somewhat knock-kneed cleric with large glasses and a brittle voice.' Later, Thomas came to think that the high colour was the result of over studying. He was given to understand that the warden was capable of giving some students a bit of a dressing down if it was necessary.

As time went on, Glyn Simon climbed up the church hierarchy. He was appointed Bishop of Swansea & Brecon in 1952 and it is said of him that when occasion required the Bishop to be a judge he could be stern, even harsh, but in general he exuded a cheerfulness and friendliness that has long been remembered by both clergy and laity. He caused controversy by describing the Gorsedd of the bards as 'having the kind of religiosity which is a dangerous thing'. He was known as a Bishop and later Archbishop who made his views known on many topical matters. He had a definite interest in other rituals of the church and was sometimes seen at the Jesuit Church in Farm Street and at the Brompton Oratory. It is not my place here to go into a deep history of Glyn's occupancy of the Bishoprics of Swansea & Brecon, and Llandaff, and ultimately the Archbishopric of Wales, but he was an outstanding man. I believe my father was at school with him and never really liked him, but father was not a classical scholar and was a great sportsman, so they were like chalk and cheese in most respects. Another great prelate of Christ College Brecon.

There have been other outstanding clergymen; Bishop Jack Thomas's son David was an excellent scholar. He was head of my father's house at Christ College and eventually, because of his deep convictions, became the Flying Bishop based in Abergavenny, who administered to those parishes and clergymen who were against women priests. Another was the Reverend Professor D P Davies, a protege of my father at Christ College, who went on, in the early part of the 20th Century, to be chairman of governors and had a huge following in many parts of the world, especially in South Korea, while he held his professorship at Lampeter. He was one of the College's great theologians and in many ways, one of the senior figures who, for many years, held St David's Lampeter and its great theology department together.

Today, as the author is a 3rd Order Franciscan, he should mention Jamie Hacker Hughes, brother of Sir Simon Hughes, who was one of the senior physiologists in the army and now is the Minister Provincial for the European Province of the Anglican 3rd Order of St Francis. Jamie is particularly motivated to review the order and make it part of the 21st century. Another of Christ College's dynamic religious sons.

References:
'Glyn Simon, His Life & Opinions' by Owain W Jones, (Gomer Press Wales 1981)
'Carnhuanawc Country, Thomas Price, A Hero For All Time', by Alan Jobbins (Wales 2000)
'Thomas Coke 1747-1814', (A Commemorative weekend to mark the 200th Anniversary of the Death of the Revd Dr Thomas Coke (Wales 2014)

LT JIM JONES

THE MILITARY AT CHRIST COLLEGE

In this book it is not my intention to write a studied history of Christ College and the military because Glenn Horridge has recently written a tome of war, '*Christ College Brecon 1914-1918*'. The most important gentleman from that era I shall be writing about is David Cuthbert Thomas, who reminds me so much of the young officers in my time in the Royal Regiment of Wales, and after all, he did belong to one of the preceding regiments of the present day Royal Welch; in fact, he was in the Royal Welch Fusiliers. Others, I shall talk about are David Price, pre. the 1st World War, my own godfather, Jim Jones, who won the Military Cross in the 2nd World War and Clive Dytor a present governor, who won the Military Cross in the Falklands. In the 1st World War, military honours won by old boys include twenty-three Military Crosses, three of which were with bar.

David Price was the eldest of five children born in Merthyr Cynog where his father had been curate since 1758. After his father died, he was offered a free place at Christ College, Brecon where the headmaster, the Rev. David Griffith had been his father's former rector. After performing well at classics, David was awarded a scholarship to Jesus College, Cambridge. But even on his way to university he spent extravagantly and despite coaxing money out of his relatives, he eventually found himself 'down and out'. He saw an advertisement while he was at the *Green Man and Still*, an inn in Oxford Street, inviting all spirited young men to enlist in the East India Company, and thus volunteered as a private soldier. Whilst waiting to board the ship to India he was horrified by the atmosphere of debauchery and vice that prevailed at the port. Luckily, he was later rescued from the ranks, and supported as an officer cadet by the naval surgeon, Thomas Evans, a relation. Evans had previously rescued John Lloyd, another private soldier, in the same way. The latter then arranged for Price also to be accepted as an officer cadet.

When Price arrived in India he was attached to an infantry regiment and soon, in action off Ceylon, won some valuable prize money which he soon lost in the boredom of the rainy season at gambling, cards and horses. Initially, he had some luck on the battlefield, two musket balls just missing him, but in 1791 during the Siege of Darwar he was wounded and lost a leg.

He was now posted to various staff jobs and began to study Persian extensively. Thus he was appointed Persian translator to General James Stuart. David was then promoted captain and in 1795 he achieved the important position of Judge Advocate of the Bombay Army. In 1799 he had secured such a reputation for integrity that he was appointed one of the seven prize agents during the campaign to capture Seringpatam, Tipu Sultan's capital. The official booty amounted to a huge sum of which Price's share as prize agent was about £400,000. David Price was promoted to major in 1804 and then went home on leave, staying the winter and spring with friends in London and finally reached Brecon in June 1806 after an absence of twenty-nine years. He married, in April 1807, the daughter of a kinswoman and moved to Watton House where he lived for the rest of his life.

After six months Price resigned his commission. He subsequently held many public positions, including Bailiff of Brecon, magistrate, and deputy-lieutenant of the county. He spent much of his time devoted to Oriental studies and wrote a series of books concerning Islamic and Indian culture and history; he was also recognised as one of the leading Oriental scholars of his day. A renowned translator of Persian, in 1830 he received the Gold Medal of the Oriental Translation Committee. When he died on 16th December 1835, he was held in such high standing that all the gentry balls were cancelled. To some, however, he was the 'jolly old major' who, at social events, was 'drunk as usual'. He left seventy-three rare manuscripts to the Royal Asiatic Society, and the sons of Walter Wilkins were left £6,000.

DAVID CUTHBERT THOMAS

A hundred years ago last March 2nd Lt David Cuthbert Thomas met his untimely death outside Fricort in the Somme, shot in the throat as he led a team repairing barbed wire defences late at night on 18th March 1916 under an almost full moon. Struggling for breath, he stoically walked back along the track which led to the advanced dressing station known as the citadel, less than a mile from the front line, by himself. As a result of his wound, the damaged tissues in his neck began to swell, blocking his airways. Thomas was instructed by the surgeon not to raise his head, his apparent disregard for this advice causing the haemorrhage that was to end his life before a tracheotomy could be performed on him.

Affectionately known to Sassoon as '*my little Tommy*', he, in his time in the regiment, had been brought into association with Sassoon, Robert Graves and Bernard Adams. Sassoon was devastated by Thomas's death and it initiated the period in Sassoon's time at the front when he used to go out into 'No Man's Land' to avenge the deaths of his friends and became known by his men as 'mad dog Sassoon'. Soon afterwards he won his MC for acknowledged bravery. His poetry at the time reflected his huge regard for Thomas and his subsequent loss. Sassoon, Graves and Adams created a powerful image of a beautiful male youth mutilated and annihilated by the political passions of the time. Sassoon in particular fell in love with the golden qualities of Thomas, although he perceived the younger officer as a heterosexual. Sassoon fell for Thomas's languid gaze, young athletic body and beautiful temperament. Thomas could be described as an aesthete, having artistic and musical as well as literary interests.

He came from a rectory as his father, Evan Thomas, was Rector of Llanedy. In school, he had joined the hostel at the age of 11. He was a popular figure, and a keen sportsman, playing in the rugby football XV, the hockey X1 and the cricket X1. He was a school prefect, editor of The Breconian and had hopes of going to Oxford. However, within a few weeks of leaving school he enlisted and joined the ranks of the 4th Public Schools Battalion. He later gained a commission into the Royal Welch Fusiliers where he formed friendships with Siegfried Sassoon and Robert Graves, who after his death memorialised him forever in their poetry. It was a wasted life with so much positive future in front of it.

He was of a generation of Christ College boys who were prepared to give their life for their country, and so often did. In his time at Christ College he established a close platonic relationship with his house master Canon A E Donaldson; he often found strength from mixing with older people. His character traits were of natural empathy, courteousness and cheerful good humour. Although a sportsman, he did not exhibit traces of competitiveness or aggression. His mother, Ethelinda often referred to him alliteratively as 'her cheerful, chattering chaffinch'. What a waste of a beautiful youth and friend.

His great friend Sassoon wrote the day after his death:

"Tonight I saw his shrouded form laid in the earth – Robert Graves beside me with his white whimsical face twisted and grieving.

Once we could not hear the solemn words for the noise of a machine-gun along the line; and when all was finished a canister fell a hundred yards away and burst with a crash.

So Tommy left us, a gentle soldier, perfect and without stain. And so he will remain in my heart, fresh and happy and brave."

The 2 following poems were written about Thomas, the first by Sassoon a week before Thomas's death, and the second by Graves.

A Subaltern – by Siegfried Sassoon

"He turned to me with his kind, sleepy gaze
And fresh face slowly brightening to the grin
That sets my memory back to summer days,
With twenty runs to make, and last man in.
He told me he'd been having a bloody time
In trenches, crouching for the crumps to burst,
While squeaking rats scampered across the slime
And the grey palsied weather did its worst.

But as he stamped and shivered in the rain,
My stale philosophies had served him well;
Dreaming about his girl had sent his brain
Blanker than ever - she'd no place in Hell....
'Good God!' he laughed, and slowly filled his pipe,
Wondering 'why he always talked such tripe'."

Not Dead – by Robert Graves

"*Walking through trees to cool my heat and pain,*
I know that David's with me here again.
All that is simple, happy, strong, he is.
Caressingly I stroke
Rough bark of the friendly oak.
A brook goes bubbling by: the voice is his.
Turf burns with pleasant smoke;
I laugh at chaffinch and at primroses.
All that is simple, happy, strong, he is.
Over the whole wood in a little while
Breaks his slow smile."

JIM JONES

With regard to the 2nd World War, my godfather, Jim Jones, was a decorated soldier who came from a Welsh farming family and whose family on his mother's side, the Richards, were the founders of the famous Criban stud of mountain ponies. His uncle, Llewellyn Richards was at Christ College, I believe, with my grandfather, Dr Tom Morgan, and he went on to win a Military Cross in the Lancers in the 1st World War. Jim's father was an old 1st World War captain, so he had a background of army in his family.

Jim went to Christ College which he didn't enjoy at all. On his 18th birthday, he joined the Young Soldiers Battalion Regular Army known as the 70th Battalion and went on to the Officer Cadet Training Unit at Morecambe. He got his commission in the South Wales Borderers but applied to join the 2nd Punjabs whose commander was Colonel Fly, a family friend. He was posted to a camp called Chittagonge near upper Burma and was in the 7th Division when the 'Japs' launched a huge attack on them, driving a wedge between the 7th and 5th Divisions. There was an area called *The Box,* held by the British, which was essentially to house the staff and administration of the British divisions, but they were put to the sword by the Japanese. By the time the divisions had stood against the Japanese, they had scored the first major British Indian victory against the enemy and inflicted 7,000 dead on them.

Jim was involved in much fighting and at one stage, started to run up a slope in front of his soldiers. He said, 'A Jap appeared on my left some five yards away – I shot him dead from the hip. I was shooting from the hip at other Japanese as more were coming at me. I was out of ammunition, so I pulled out two grenades which I threw in front of me. The grenades held the Japs back for a time, but two very brave Sepoys rushed forward and dragged me back after I had experienced a terrific pain in my ribs and fallen to the ground. It transpired at the end of the battle that I'd run into 160 Japs and four light machine guns in a large bunker.' Jim was pulled off his stretcher because there was such a shortage of them. It was after this action that Jim was awarded an immediate Military Cross. In the citation it was said that after only nine weeks in India, Lt David Howell Jones (Jim), 2nd Punjabs, was posted to Arakan and won the MC for what was described in the citation as one of the most outstanding cases of gallantry through the past six months campaign. He personally led an attack against the Japanese position in the face of automatic and grenade fire. He was severely wounded, but his men continued and took ten yards of vital ground which led to the success of a subsequent full-scale attack with tanks.

Jim is now about 94 years old, still blessed with a twinkle in his eye, and like so many of that generation takes joy in everyday existence, having survived the war. As my godfather, he was always very supportive, although I was lucky to get a box of handkerchiefs for Christmas, while my brother, whose two godfathers were Lord Brecon and the Rev David Isitt, chaplain of Kings College Cambridge, got such presents as *The Oxford History of England!* Jim married Gwen Horton, from a well-known Wiltshire farming family, and they were married for fifty one years. He was always a good horseman, and an entrepreneur in farming terms. My father was his best man and he, like so many of my father's friends had the Military Cross, which inspired me to go into the army.

CLIVE I DYTOR (SHB, 68-74)

Clive I Dytor (SHB, 68-74) Falklands War hero, entered the Church after being awarded the Military Cross. He was a troop commander in 45 Commando and his award for gallantry came in recognition of his heroism during the ferocious fighting in the Battle of Two Sisters during the Falklands War thirty years ago.

In June 1982, he and his troop: 8 Troop, Zulu Company found themselves in a desperate situation early in the morning whilst attempting to capture the heavily defended ridge. Totally exposed on the lower slopes, they were being shot at by the enemy with a 50 Browning machine gun, killing three marines and seriously injuring one. Another marine was killed despite artillery fire being called in to destroy the machine gun crew. It was Dytor's next courageous action which earned him his Military Cross. Realising they were running out of ammunition, he bravely and somewhat recklessly ran on his own up the slope shouting the company battle cry, 'Zulu, Zulu, Zulu!' His stunned marines then followed him and when his rifle jammed he automatically dropped down on one knee and managed to clear the stoppage, saving himself from almost certainly being hit, while his troop carried on ruthlessly, moving from enemy bunker to enemy bunker, clearing the positions as they went, finally capturing the machine gun and killing the crew.

The battle raged in the dark for several hours until, nearing Port Stanley, they were ordered to halt in case they were mistaken for the enemy. The assault was planned as part of a huge operation to break the Argentinians will to fight. After the battle was over and the enemy had surrendered, Clive Dytor took stock; he had joined the Royal Marines two years earlier after graduating from Cambridge and it was while he was in hospital shortly after the Falklands War had ended, having broken his leg playing rugby, that he was able to plan what he really wanted to do, and that was to go into the Church. Four years later he trained for the priesthood at Wycliffe Hall, Oxford and became chaplain at Tonbridge School in Kent.

He believes his conversion to Catholicism began when he read John Henry Newman's autobiography describing his spiritual journey from the Church of England to Rome. Eight years later he swam the Tiber and was granted the Oratory headship at the school in Reading founded by Cardinal Newman. He instils in his boys the qualities of commitment, loyalty and tenacity, as embodied by the military.

Born in Cardiff in 1956, Clive Dytor was educated at Christ College, Brecon and was a prefect and a member of the 1st XV. He flourished in this environment, was a popular member of the school and noted for his mild eccentricities. Married for twenty-six years, his wife still doesn't know exactly what he did in the

Falklands.

PETER WATKINS

WRITERS, ACTORS AND FILM DIRECTORS

Theophilus Jones

Theophilus Jones was born in Brecon on 18th October 1759. On 8th November he was baptised in the Chapel of St Mary in that town. His father was, at that time, curate of St David's Brecon and lived in a charming old house in Lion Street. The future historian passed some of his early years at Llywn Einon, his grandfather's house and young though he was, there can be little doubt that his antiquarian tastes were awakened and fostered by his grandfather.

He was educated at Christ College, Brecon, which was then a large and flourishing school, attended by the sons of the surrounding country gentry. During the time he was there, the headmaster was the Rev David Griffith, an accomplished scholar, of whom Theophilus spoke in after years as 'the respected and respectable preceptor of my youth.' It was decided he would become a lawyer and he was articled to Mr Penoyre Watkins, a solicitor, with a well-established practice, then living in Brecon. After his articles, he practised successfully as a solicitor and attorney in his county town. A vacancy occurring in the Deputy Registrarship of the Archdeaconry of Brecon, he was appointed to that office which he held until his death.

On their marriage, Mr and Mrs Theophilus Jones lived in a large and comfortable house in Mount Street, Brecon, now converted into an inn known as The George Hotel. When his father died, he moved into his house in Lion Street. He was not altogether unbiased as an historian as is shown by his ignoring the martyrdom of John Penry, previously described in this book, and the life work of Dr Thomas Coke. He is said, also, not to have appreciated Henry Vaughan, the silurist's, poems. It could be said, however, that he was a better historian than a literary critic. His history of Breconshire is still one of the standard histories, and the original editions are hugely sought after by people today. Jones's history of the county of Brecknock was published in two volumes in Brecon in 1805 and 1809. It was reprinted in one volume in 1898 and then in a considerably enlarged form in four volumes edited by Joseph Russell Bailey (1st Baron Glanusk 1909-30). His memory lives on in his books, and his memorial is up in the chapel in Christ College, Brecon.

References:
'Theophilus Jones, FSA, Historian: 'His Life, Letters & Literary Remains' by Edwin Davies (Leopold Classic Library reprinted from 1905 original, Wales).

Jonathan Smith

In much more modern times, Jonathan Smith has become an acclaimed writer and novelist. Jonathan, I remember as an excellent cricketer, as was his brother David, both in my father's house, Donaldson's in Christ College. Smith was born in Gloucestershire to a family of teachers originally from the Rhondda Valley and he read English at St John's College, Cambridge. Smith took up his first teaching job at Loretto School in Scotland. Then, after a brief stint at Melbourne Grammar School in Australia, he taught at Tunbridge School, UK for the rest of his career and was head of English for seventeen years. His former pupils at Tunbridge include political historian and biographer Sir Anthony Seldon, novelist Bik Ramseth, poet Christopher Reid and actor Dan Stevens.

Smith's son, Ed, was his former pupil at Tunbridge and a former cricketer for England. Jonathan's first novel *'Wilfred and Eileen'* was adapted for BBC television into a four part serial. He also wrote the screenplay for the film adaptation of *'Summer in February'*, starring Dominic Cooper, Emily

Browning and Dan Stevens, which was released in June 2013. His latest novel, *'Churchill's Secret KBO'* was adapted for a feature length film starring Michael Gambon, which was screened around Christmas 2015 on ITV. He has written over twenty plays, two autobiographical accounts and seven novels.

Peter Watkins

Peter Watkins was born on 29th October 1935 in Norberton, Surrey. He is described as an English film and television director, although having been sent to a Welsh school and with a name like Watkins he probably had some Welsh blood. He has lived in Sweden, Canada and Lithuania in past years, and now lives in France. He is one of the pioneers of 'docudrama' and his films present radical and pacifist ideas in a non-traditional style. The first of his films was *'Culloden'*, which portrayed the Jacobite uprising of 1745 in a documentary style as if television reporters were interviewing the participants and accompanying them into battle. His biographical film *'Edward Munch la Commune'* re-enacts the Paris commune days using a large cast of French non actors.

Watkins went to Christ College, Brecon where he had a slightly ambivalent attitude to the school and went on to do National Service with the East Surrey Regiment, followed by studying acting at the Royal Academy of Dramatic Art. His reputation as a political provocateur was amplified by *'Punishment Park'*, a story of violent political conflict in the United States, which coincided with the Kent State Massacre in Ohio in 1970. Opposition to war is a common theme to his work, but the films' political messages are often ambiguous, usually allowing the main characters to present violently opposing viewpoints, which in many cases are improvised by the cast.

Watkins is also known for political statements about the film and TV media, writing extensively about flaws in television news and the dominance of the Hollywood derived narrative style that he describes as 'the monoform'. His great film, *'The War Game'* was banned for twenty years, but when it was released, was acclaimed as a huge contribution to the nuclear war debate. His influence reached far and wide. Sighting their 1969 'Bed in' and 'Peace' concerts, an interviewer asked John Lennon and Yoko Ono 'Is there any one particular incident that got you started in this peace campaign?' John answered, 'What really struck it off was a letter we got from a guy called Peter Watkins who made a film called '*The War Game.*' Peter said, 'People in your position have a responsibility to use the world media for peace', and we sat on the letter for about three weeks thinking, well, we're doing our best. All you need is love, man. That letter just sort of sparked it all off; it was like getting your induction papers for peace.'

Hubert Rees

The next person in this chapter is the larger than life character Hubert Rees. He appeared in a cameo part in '*Tiger Bay*' in the 50s in his early acting career. He always found parts in '*Under Milk Wood*' where, in one staging, Rachel Roberts had to tell him off for being late on stage. He acted at Stratford as the villain Cymbeline. He was an ardent cricketer and was a great supporter of cricket and rugby matches between Llandovery and Brecon. One story tells how he stayed with Oliver Reid at Lord Bath's in Longleat, but they were sent home after painting an indiscreet message on the lawn. I went to his funeral, where Kate O'Mara read one lesson, and Windsor Davies read the other. He was held in high esteem in the acting world, was great fun to be with, and a great character.

Jamie Owen

Jamie Owen, the television presenter, was well known throughout Wales as anchor man of '*Wales Today*'. He was born in Haverfordwest in Pembrokeshire. His father, James Meyrick Owen was a Pembroke Dock solicitor and his mother was a health visitor and midwife. He was educated at Pennar School, Pembroke Dock, Christ College, Brecon, The University of

Gloucester and Cardiff University. Owen joined the BBC in 1986 and worked at BBC Radio 3, later joining BBC Radio 4 as a newsreader and announcer. He was a continuity announcer for BBC1 and BBC2 Wales in the early 1990s and has been a main presenter of BBC Wales' flagship news programme '*BBC Wales Today* ' since 1994. Jamie has also presented a weekday morning radio show on BBC Radio Wales and has been working with BBC Wales Service Trust in the Middle East, in Jordan, Libya and Egypt. The author regularly sees him in the Griffin Inn, Felinfach with his lovely friend Susannah and was very impressed by his eulogy to Kelvin Redford at the latter's funeral where he described his great affection for Kelvin and all he had taught him at Christ College, Brecon.

In terms of entrepreneurship, I must mention here 'Pop up Opera', an innovative touring opera company which aims to broaden the appeal of opera and to challenge the way opera is performed by taking it into unusual spaces and making it intimate and engaging. These locations include a boat, a cylindrical shaft beneath the Thames, a cider barn, a winery, and even a 100ft underground candle lit cavern. The company was founded by Clementine Lovell, an old Christ College girl, in 2011. It was built from scratch and has grown from an initial twelve performances to ninety performances a year with three to four different productions over three seasons.

Roscoe Howells   1919-2014

Obituary from the Pembrokeshire Historical Society by Christopher Gilham

The passing, at the age of 94 of our Vice-President, Roscoe Howells, has deprived Pembrokeshire of one of its great characters.

William Herbert Roscoe Howells, to give him his full name, was born in Bethany Manse, Saundersfoot, on 27th October 1919. He was educated in Saundersfoot CP School, Tenby CP

School and Christ College, Brecon.

Roscoe began his working life as a dairy farmer but he was a man of many talents and diverse interests. His numerous achievements and offices illustrate this. He was founder member Pembrokeshire Records Society and former Chairman of Pembrokeshire Historical Society. He was a member of the Pembrokeshire County Committee of RABI from 1955 and became President of Pembrokeshire County Agricultural Society in 1977.

Roscoe represented Amroth on Narberth RDC, 1952-57 and served as Hon. Clerk to Amroth Parish Council. He was Secretary of Amroth United Reformed Church, Chairman of Pembrokeshire Football League and Vice-President of Glamorgan County Cricket Club. He founded Amroth Juniors football team and was President of St. Helen's Balconiers. He took part in amateur dramatics and played the ukulele.

This is only a selection of Roscoe's many and varied interests and offices and he is remembered with affection by those he met through them. However, his main impact came through his writing and media work. He wrote six novels, all set in Pembrokeshire, and sixteen works of non-fiction, together with numerous articles. He was a frequent broadcaster on radio and television.

Roscoe was not afraid of controversy and was always ready to stand up for those causes he held dear. He could use an easy tone in journalism and many will remember him masquerading as a gossipy Pembrokeshire woman in "Over the Garden Wall" with his catch-phrase, "There t'is then".

Roscoe was happily married to Lucie but knew the pain of widowhood. However, he was blessed by a second happy marriage to Margaret. He leaves a son, Kevin, and grandson, Simon.

In mature years Roscoe joined the Roman Catholic Church, a decision partially influenced by his great love of Caldey. One of my best memories of him comes from that island. He was leading a small group on a tour. We thought we were alone when, suddenly, a woman's voice carried to us, 'Roscoe, come here you naughty boy!' We were rather surprised but then saw the lady holding a small boy by the hand. One of us asked how she had come to give the child that rather uncommon name. 'I named him after the famous author, Roscoe Howells', she replied and explained how Roscoe's books has inspired her and her husband with a deep love of Pembrokeshire.

Roscoe was delighted.

And here was his genius. He was a mature man who had always kept a bit of the 'naughty boy' about him and who, with the total commitment and enthusiasm of the child, could inspire others to a love of the county which he held so dear.

Paul G Brown

Another famous old boy whom the school didn't know much about was P G Brown. This from his obituary:

Paul Brown, the opera and theatre designer, who has died aged 57, was a dealer in truth and beauty; his great talent, in a career crammed with landmark productions, was to point up the difference between the two.

There was always the moment in a Paul Brown show where the audience gasped; the flaming staircase at the end of Pelléas et Mélisande (Glyndebourne, 2004), the carnival of giant rutting rabbits in The Fairy Queen (Glyndebourne, 2009). Sometimes the show was one extended coup de théâtre. The Tempest (2000), where Ariel dived through dark waters on the flooded stage of the Almeida, was described in the Guardian as the most inventive staging of Shakespeare since Peter Brook's A Midsummer Night's Dream. The 2009 Aida, on the lake stage at Bregenz, upped the ante with speeding gun-boats and a sky-ballet of shipyard cranes.

Paul was my friend for nearly 40 years, and I never knew him to repeat an idea. Yet for all the fabulous invention, there was a scrupulousness to Paul's character and creativity that rejected spectacle for spectacle's sake. Nor was he swayed by audience expectation; he could do "ravishing" like no one else (as evidenced by his 2006 Tosca at the Royal Opera House) but inclined, often, towards the ravaged. Working up designs for La Traviata in Verona (2004), he knew very well that the amphitheatre crowd liked its Violettas piped in meringue. He gave them a bald and battered whore and took an extra kick at populist sentiment with a shrine of cellophaned flowers.

Paul was fast and very funny, charming enough to convince the grandest divas they would look marvellous in a chicken suit, or dragging a chandelier, on their knees, through mud. His period costumes were exquisite and always authentic; he could tell you, to the month, when a stock or a stomacher was first worn, but ducked the dead hand of historicism with forensic attention to character.

It was entirely fitting that his Oscar-nominated costume designs for the 1995 film Angels and Insects turned on the notion of clothing-as-carapace, a notion which later found apotheosis in the gorgeous, glinting bugs that shimmied from behind the fridge in Rameau's Hippolyte et Aricie (Glyndebourne, 2013). The modern "clothes, not costumes" mantra bounced off Paul. "It doesn't really cut it," he pointed out, "when you're making a frock-coat for a beetle."

He micromanaged sets to an astonishing degree. Staging Coriolanus and Richard II in the derelict Gainsborough Studios in 2000, Paul was excited to find a number of old doors, richly textured with guano. Informed that this was a technical bio-hazard, he allowed the doors to be washed, but each individual splatter was painted back on by hand.

Paul enjoyed unusually close collaborations with directors, and worked predominantly with Graham Vick and Jonathan Kent; Vick remembers "an incredibly powerful intellect and personality". Kent compares the director/designer relationship to a marriage. "We had a long-running stand-off over Wellington boots." he recalls, "I kept banning them, Paul kept sneaking them in. For 20 years."

Born in Cowbridge, Vale of Glamorgan, the son of Alan Brown, a master printer, and his wife, Enfys (nee Jones), Paul was educated at Christ college, Brecon, and at the University of St Andrews, where he took an MA in English literature. Student drama in the early 1980s was a drab "black box and hessian" affair. Paul tore down the hemp and swathed the college theatre in cloth-of-gold, most notably for a staggeringly precocious production of Dryden's Amphitryon (baroque to his soul, Paul loved nothing better than a deus ex machina).

His talent was nurtured by Malcolm Edwards, a London director then working in St Andrews, and soon Paul was moonlighting in West End shows. Friends stuck doggedly to the narrative, in lectures and tutorials, that Paul was "just parking, and would be along presently", but the gaff was blown when, in his final term, he arrived to register for exams in the English department; barely acquainted with the building, he swept, rather grandly, into a broom cupboard (and was too embarrassed to come out).

On graduating, he studied stage design with Margaret "Percy" Harris at the Riverside Studios, London, and after an indecently short period in fringe theatre, flipped into the fast-stream. Rarely sleeping, fuelled by Nescafé and pastry, he was unimaginably prolific. In 2004 alone, Paul had 21 separate operas playing in the UK, Verona, Chicago, Paris, New York, Sydney, Madrid, Bologna, Amsterdam and San Francisco. In 2013 he won the Royal Designer for Industryaward for his role in fostering UK set and costume design on the world stage.

In his late 30s, Paul found great happiness with Andy Cordy, an artist, and they celebrated their civil partnership in 2006. They lived in a 15th-century manor house in Pembrokeshire with assorted poultry, and dogs called Merkin and Fecal. ("They're Welsh names," Paul always assured interested, non-Welsh children.) The creative hub was a London basement, thick with fumes from spray-mount and lined with glowing jars of pigment like an alchemist's cell. Costume-drawings, which he often undertook in bed, were a form of meditation for Paul; worked up in coloured pencil line by line and layer by layer, sketches took on the depth and shine of silk, velvet or feathers. Pencils reduced to stubs were honourably retired to the Tin of the Little Heroes.

Paul was diagnosed with cancer in December 2015. He

worked, as he wished, to the end. It is hard for so many of his friends to think there will be no more calls pinging in from airport lounges around the world, starting, always, with the same, Peter Pan crow ("It's me!") and ending in a firework spatter of farewells ("Bye now, bye-bye, bye ... bye"). Paul was not only the most influential stage designer of his generation, and a generous mentor, but also an extravagant gift of a friend.

Paul is survived by Andy, his mother and his sister, Jane.

• Paul Gareth Brown, stage designer, born 13 May 1960; died 13 November 2017

LORD ATKIN

LORD ATKIN

James Richard Atkin always thought of himself as a Welshman, although he had Irish, Welsh and Australian origins. Having been born in Brisbane, Australia, the eldest of three sons, his mother brought him and his siblings back to her own mother's house 'Pantlludw', on the river Dovey in Wales. He went away to school at the age of 8 to the Friars' School in Bangor. His headmaster there, Mr Lloyd, moved to Christ College, Brecon in 1878 and Atkin went with him. This old school, with a high academic tradition established a permanent place in Atkin's affections. Lloyd was an outstanding teacher and headmaster.

The school was in a poor condition when Lloyd arrived, with only a single form of no more than ten or eleven boys but within a few years it had 100 boys and was regularly taking scholarships at Oxford and Cambridge. When Atkin returned in 1913 to give out prizes, he told the boys, 'There is a definition of a philanthropist as 'someone who made two blades of grass grow where one grew before', and if that was the proper definition of a philanthropist, did that not apply to a man like Lloyd who created three great schools in his career?' Atkin also spoke of moral courage, 'There was one thing the boys ought to learn while at school which was in the domain of language. If they learned at school when to say 'no', they would have learnt one of the great lessons of their life.'

From Brecon, Atkin went up to Magdalene at the age of 17. Oxford, however, was not the happiest period of his life. As he later conceded, he was too young and the college too full of the well-to-do for him to gain confidence quickly. The indifferent health which dogged his later life first became apparent at that time, and he was disappointed to miss, by the narrowest margin, a 1st in Classical Moderations and Greats.

Atkin was known for his humanity as a judge, which did not spring from an original moral code, although he was a devotee and committed Christian. He had no time for 'churchiness' or sanctimony. He was always aware of the commerce of daily life and this, perhaps, was one of the main features of his compassion. His compassionate understanding was seen in his great contributions in his debates in the Lords on the Marriage Bill in 1937. Thus, he became one of the greatest of all British common lawyers, asking the question in Donaghue v Stevenson 'Who then in law is my neighbour?' which became the foundation of the whole modern law of negligence. His courageous dissent in the wartime detention case of Liversidge v Anderson is now recognised as an historic stand on principle.

Atkin married Lizzie Hemmant in 1893 after a five year engagement and had six daughters and two sons, the elder son being killed in the 1st World War. His daughter Rosaline became a barrister at Gray's Inn while the fourth daughter, Nancy, (to her father's delight) became an actress. Atkin enjoyed the music hall and was fond of entertaining at their various town homes in Kensington with musical evenings. He spent every summer with his family in Aberdovey, where he enjoyed tennis, golf and bridge. He was a popular man in that community and was paraded through the village on a hand drawn cab on his appointment to the High Court. When possible, he sat as a Justice of the Peace in Towyn and Machynlleth and eventually chaired the Merioneth Quarter Sessions. He died of bronchitis in Aberdovey, where he was buried.

From 1928 until his death he was a Lord of Appeal in Ordinary under the title of Baron Atkin of Aberdovey in the County of Merioneth. He was always strongly motivated by his Christian faith and relied upon testing the law against the demands of common sense and the interest of the ordinary working man. He would come to a settled view early on in hearing a case, and as a Law Lord his colleagues often found him indefatigable in his opinions and difficult to persuade as to the merits of alternative views.

48

There have been about fifteen Lord Atkin Lectures at Christ College to commemorate the great judge. These, for the most part, were arranged by Leolin Price QC, a distinguished chancery lawyer and son-in-law of Lord Brecon, who, as a governor, had great affection for the school and arranged for some great names to come down and give the lecture, including Lord Owen (whose father had been at Christ College), the Rt Hon Dominic Grieve, The Rt Hon Lord Bingham of Cornhill and Sir Simon Hughes. These high quality lectures give the pupils in the school an insight into some of our top legal brains.

Latterly, Jonathan Arter has made the arrangements; he was the author's best friend at Christ College and comes from a well-known local family in Breconshire. His father was a boxing blue and naval chaplain and eventually Vicar of Llandew; his mother, a very talented lady, was very much involved in the arts in Breconshire. Jonathan, a very able lawyer in his own right, became chairman of the Welsh Law Society, and with Paul Silk, and the author, were the Latin and Classical 6th form in the late 1960s.

References:
'Lord Atkin' by Geoffrey Lewis (Butterworths) London 1983

JAMES DICKSON INNES

TWO FAMOUS ARTISTS

In the author's time at Christ College there was a very bohemian head of art called Mr Bell, who lived in the middle of the wood on the hill opposite Llanspyddid. He was given to riding his large motor bike back to Scotland and encouraged many people in the trade of fine art. However, Christ College's two greater sons who were grand artists were the following:

James Dickson Innes 1887-1914

In autumn 1898, from a family that was originally Scottish, James followed his brothers to Christ College, Brecon in 1898. There is no record that he distinguished himself academically, but his art suggests that on the train to and from Llanelli and Brecon, at least a dozen times a year for six years, he observed in all seasons, at different times of day, how variations in light transformed landscape. The school had a fine academic record, and by 1902, James aged 15 was the only Innes boy remaining at Christ College. He left Brecon at Easter 1904, and in the same year his name was enrolled at the Carmarthen School of Art. After a year of study at Carmarthen, Innes returned to S W Wales for more landscape work.

Following in the footsteps of Turner, he painted Carew Castle, Pembroke, Chepstow, Tintern and Ludlow and later, Carreg Cennen. He enrolled initially for three terms at the Slade School of Fine Art in London. His mother had accompanied her son to London, for she was already concerned about his health. Innes's first term at the Slade placed him in the presence of a group of accomplished and influential painters at the heart of contemporary art in London. The group from the Slade included his teachers, Steer and Tonks, and very significantly would turn out another Welsh painter, Augustus John. Innes would have been dazzled by the exploits and glamour of his fellow Welshman.

In February 1907, Innes was 20 and had been at the Slade for over eighteen months. He was adopted by a wealthy Bostonian, Edward Perry Warren, who sponsored him as an artist. In October 1907 he returned for his last year at the Slade; his address given in the NAEC autumn catalogue was 125, Cheyne Walk. Innes first met John in the autumn of 1907 and was fully dazzled. He wasn't considered a great success at the Slade but his social life was extending, and his charm and politeness made him popular; he was introduced to a number of socialites like Horace de Vere Cole and Lord Howard de Walden who later became his close supportive friends.

He had an all excelling sense of colour, which he applied in particular to the landscape of Wales. While he needed the stimulus of friends, his fellow artists and the London exhibitions to shape his art, his health needed clean air and a regular regime. London's smoky, foggy atmosphere combined to bring on the next of a series of health breakdowns, so he was persuaded to leave London and relinquish the teaching engagement he had taken on at the Slade. After the death of his grandmother, and his and his mother's sojourn at St Ives, they took up temporary lodging at Calstock, north of Plymouth.

Innes later went over to France, like so many of his contemporaries and his stay in Paris transformed his life. He met the lady of his dreams in Paris, one Euphebia, born Nina Forrest, married to Henry Lamb. According to John, she was the love of Innes's life, the lady of his dreams. He also spent some time on his 1910 trip reconnoitring the beautiful area to the north and south of Collioure on the Mediterranean coast.

In 1911, he got together with John who encouraged his first one man show at Jack Knew Stubbs's Chenil Gallery. To provide the pictures, Innes had gone on a wild Wales tour. He moved inland to tackle the mountains, taking the road from Carmarthen to Beddgelert, where Mynydd Mawr appears as 'Thunder in the Mountains'. He was looking for the great natural sites, like waterfalls and mountains such as *Siabod*. In

North Wales he learned how to capture the essence of what he had felt in the mountains; the brooding melancholy, their rugged features and the changing light. His exhibition '*Landscapes*' in 1911 opened about a month before his 21st birthday and was a great success. Also in 1911, he set out with John for a tour of north Wales where Innes particularly loved the *Arenig* peaks. For a long time he had worked with water colour and pen, but with John's help, he discovered a new way of working in oil which was to transform his work. They lived quite a bohemian life in North Wales, mixing with the locals and sometimes falling in love with the odd gypsy girl.

He had a second show in 1912 in the Chenil Gallery; again, it was successful with the new technique in painting by Innes going down well. Back in London during the autumn of 1912 and using John's studio in Chelsea, Innes began new work based on his recent expedition to Ireland. But by this time, his health was deteriorating; he was so low that he seemed incapable of getting out of bed in the morning without a stiff dose of brandy. His illness was tuberculosis. His body suffered from it while his creative faculty was at its peak. His strength would recover temporarily, which allowed him to go over to France again, and then he began to prepare for his 3rd one man show at the Chenil. Augustus John's support at this stage of Innes's life was crucial to the young man's well- being as the person who also had bailed him out in 1910 when Innes's allowance was stopped. John had then taken on the mantle of agent, promoting Innes's work and reserving pictures for his own patron, Quinn to buy. In the last week of August 1914, Innes died. Cole's heartfelt eulogy at the funeral said:

'*He loved the mountains, and the spaces*
Where breakers curl along a desert shore,
Great suns, and women's magic-making faces
Aglow amidst some vineyard's trellised store'
He loved all things where beauty is most wild,
His soul a poet and his heart a child.

The storm-girl summits of his native land
Made mountain music that to him was speech;
He learnt their secrets; and a flaming brand,
Born of their vapours, wisp-like out of reach,
Lured him to seek out beauty in the woods
That crown with purple those wild solitudes.'

His death was eclipsed by the reports of the first great casualties from Flanders. But his work has been commemorated by a magnificent retrospective in the National Museum of Wales in 2014, marking the 100th anniversary of his death. The journeys to Christ College had a remarkable effect on his appreciation of landscape, even if the teaching at the school was not that encouraging for budding young artists such as Innes in his time there.

Thomas Jones 1742-1803

Jones was the second son of Thomas Jones of Trefonnen, Llandrindod Wells and his wife Hannah. He was the second of sixteen children, seven of whom died young. From 1750, he was brought up at Pencerrig near Builth Wells in a house and estate inherited by his mother. Pencerrig, the place Thomas Jones was always to regard as home, in fact belonged to John Hope and did not become the property of the Joneses until Hope's death in 1761. He was a pupil at Christ College from 1753-1758; at the same time he was under the particular care of the local dissenting minister. It was at Christ College that he first found his fondness for solitude, a theme that recurs throughout the great fund of memoirs which he left to us. He was encouraged both by a friend at school who taught him the basics of drawing, and by his father, who helped him by buying prints, drawing materials and paints. As he was the second son, he had no great expectations of inheriting Pencerrig, although his maternal great uncle did offer to pay for him to go up to Oxford. Like so many sons of the Welsh gentry, he entered Jesus College, the first Protestant foundation at Oxford which had been established in 1571 by Welshman Hugh Price. Jones dropped out of Oxford after his uncle, who was sponsoring him, died in 1761, and pursued a career as an artist.

He enrolled at William Shipley's drawing school in November 1761 and in 1763 he persuaded the leading landscape painter of the day and fellow Welshman Richard Wilson to take him on as a pupil. He was full of high spirits at the time and was sometimes censored for this. Jones always appreciated his Welsh cultural heritage but had no knowledge of the Welsh language. He clearly met with Welshmen such as William Parry in London; a close friend was the poet and critic, the Rev Evan Lloyd of Fronderw, Bala, through whom he met David Garrick and with whom he enjoyed various escapades in London.

In 1765 Jones began to exhibit at the Society of Artists, the forerunner of the Royal Academy. From 1769 onwards, his landscapes began to adopt the 'grand manner', becoming settings for scenes from literature, mythology and history. One of his best known works from this period is *'The Bard'* based on the poem by Thomas Gray. He also spent some time in Italy, where he produced a series of views of Naples. painted from 1782-83. Here, he broke with some of the conventions of classical landscape, in favour of direct observation.

He made his first visit to Naples in 1778, staying there for five months, and later returned to Rome for a time, living in a house near the Spanish Steps. He took on a Danish widow called Maria Moncke as his maidservant, forming a relationship with her. She gave birth to his two daughters in Naples. Upon hearing of his father's death in 1782 after six years in Italy, he returned to Britain with his family. He was lucky enough to inherit his father's estate in 1787 on the death of his brother Major John Jones and finally married Maria on 16th September 1789. By 1791 he was an established county figure, becoming High Sheriff of Radnorshire. He died from angina pectoris on 29th April 1803. After a retrospective exhibition in the National Museum of Wales in 2003, he has become known historically as one of Wales's most prestigious artists.

References:
'Thomas Jones 1742-1803, An Artist Rediscovered' edited by
Ann Sumner and Greg Smith (Yale University Press New
Haven and London in association with National Museums &
Galleries of Wales 2003)
'James Dickinson Innes 1887-1914' by John Hoole and
Margaret Simons, (Lund Humphries 2013)

LORD BRECON

FAMILIES AND BENEFACTORS

The Powell family were very significant in the history of Christ College, Brecon. They were descended from Alderman David Powell who was High Sheriff in 1916 and Chairman of the County Memorial Hospital. He was a JP and was awarded the MBE, and he took a prominent part in the life of Kensington Chapel for half a century. He owned the brewery in the Struet which was situated just beyond the kissing gate that leads to the Priory Groves, obviously a man imbued with a great sense of public service.

At the time of his death, Mr Powell was the senior governor of the College and for several years held the responsible position of chairman of the finance committee where his shrewd and business-like talents were of great value. All that concerned Brecon was of interest to him, and Christ College occupied a high place in his affections, as is shown by the fact that he sent both his sons there. His sons Gwyn and Idris and their cousin Hugh Stanton were all in the war and at Christ College. Idris was a regular soldier in the Welch Regiment and served in France, Ireland, Germany and China. He retired in 1937 and founded the OTC?? in Christ College and Llandovery College. In the 2nd World War he served in this country.

Hugh Stanton was a general practitioner who joined the Royal Army Medical Corps in 1939 and served in Dunkirk and later in the Chindits in Burma. He returned as a GP to Grimsby where Dr Peter Powell worked with him for many happy years as a partner. He was mentioned in dispatches following the Burma campaign.

Peter Powell was in Orchard House and School House in 1934 – 1935 when he joined the naval section of the Combined Cadet Force. He was head of school in 1942-43 and later joined

Hugh Stanton as a GP. After retiring, he became a much loved and hardworking governor of Christ College, Brecon while working part-time for the NHS. Some years later it was suggested that the new art gallery should be named after the family. His grandchildren went to Christ College and other members of the family including David Harpur, who was a great character and had the extraordinary record in the military of being decommissioned twice, once in the British army and once in the Indian army, we believe, for so-called insubordination because he tended to be very outspoken, probably at the wrong times. David said, 'The image I have of him is passing General Gattie who was leading his division on horseback in India and giving him a copy of the Brecon & Radnor Express as Gattie was a local man'.

Altogether, thirteen of the family were at Christ College, which beats my own family, the Morgans, whom I've talked about enough already.

Part of the Rich family came from Essex in 1500-1600. Richard Rich was Chancellor of England; the family were also the Earls of Warwick but did not live in the castle. Various Richs were mayors of Brecon and ten of the family were at Christ College. I particularly remember Ray Rich, a big strong man of enormous integrity who had been captured at the time of Dunkirk but was repatriated as a prisoner of war when he contracted tuberculosis. I was in school with Charlie Rich who was a very robust back row forward and later became an entrepreneur as did his brother Malcolm. We shall now go on to describe the achievements of Malcolm's two sons, Harry and David.

"Horti couture: the Rich brothers grow their name with a creation for Chanel

Design / 23 Feb 2016 / By Georgia Dehn

Harry and David Rich know their Dianthus gallicus from their Primula japonica and could talk all day about flowers

59

and plants from around the world but start a conversation about luxury fashion brands and they will tell you that they only know one, 'the French one: Chanel'.

The brothers, originally from Brecon in Wales, were commissioned by the fashion house to create a garden at its 'Mademoiselle Privé' exhibition at the Saatchi Gallery in London at the end of last year.

No previous exhibition at the Saatchi Gallery had made use of the 1,500 sq. m. approach to the Duke of York's Headquarters on King's Road, where the gallery has its base. The Rich brothers (professionally known as Rich Landscapes) would have quite liked their haute horticulture to become permanent, not least because the build was a logistical nightmare; deliveries and collections were only allowed within a one-hour window each day.

However, they are used to temporary triumphs. Last year, they took a gold medal at the Royal Horticultural Society Chelsea Flower Show, a sort of Cannes Film Festival for the green-fingered, which takes place just down the road from the Saatchi every spring, for a garden featuring a moveable shack on rails. 'You work so hard to make a space for people to enjoy and then if it is an exhibition or show garden it has to be dismantled,' says David.

The three 'garden rooms' they created for the 'Mademoiselle Privé' exhibition represented key influences in Coco Chanel's life, including her lover and muse, Boy Capel. 'It is a subtle interpretation,' says Harry. 'If you look at the finer details within the garden, you can see the points we were drawing on'. The hard landscaping comprised steel, charred oak and bound gravel, and the brothers cleverly wove together a chevron pattern from a Chanel handbag design with the brand's interlocking Cs. Some 200 trees and shrubs were installed, and a natural meadow knitted together the rest of the planting.

The Rich brothers would like you to believe they are simply geeky garden folk, but they have become the most fashionable thing in horticulture. The connection with Chanel has simply underscored it.

They are blessed with rugged good looks, which helps, and may well be the reason they've recently had a TV production company knocking on their door; they like to use naturalistic planting styles, which happen to be de rigueur at the moment. For the 'Mademoiselle Privé' garden they mixed up the looseness of grasses with formal hedging; and every other aspect of their creations feels like it could be the work of a stylist.

They cycle to their east London studio on 'fixies', with Harry's black Labrador, Darcy, bounding alongside. David plays guitar in a folk band in his spare time; Harry plays jazz trumpet. 'He'd rather stay at home practising than come to meetings with me,' says David. 'You can always tell when he's been practising when he does turn up, because he has geisha lips.'

Harry and David, 28 and 25 respectively, grew up in a nature-loving household. Their father was a forester before founding the peat-free compost business Vital Earth. Both boys were creative and their father helped steer them towards a career in landscape architecture. 'I graduated and started the business in 2011, which until last year was based in Wales', says Harry. 'David went off to study the same degree I did, Landscape Architecture, at what was then Leeds Metropolitan University, but spent a lot of his time helping me out.'

Last year's Chelsea Flower Show gold medal was the pair's second (they've also had a silver1-gilt), and they are the show's youngest exhibitors to have won a gold on its Main Avenue. They will have to give Chelsea a miss this year, because they are too busy. 'We are very lucky to have a wide range of work,' says David. 'We have two new big private residential projects at design stage, an organic farm in Devon and the garden of a contemporary concrete home right on the seafront in Wales.' Meanwhile, developers have brought them on board to work *on the outdoor elements of projects such as London's thirty one storey Canaletto tower. They have also been approached about the landscaping of a 500-acre site in Yangshuo, China, with a view to creating British inspired gardens. 'It is still at the early concept stage,' says David. 'The development will have boutique hotels and private residences, but seventy per cent of the space is gardens.' They are thinking of walled gardens and oak trees and have plans for a horticultural education centre on site 'to teach people about the culture of British gardening.' It's a culture they are already imparting - and with some force."*

As originally featured in the March 2016 issue of Wallpaper* (W*204)

Jack Rees, Major Harold John Valentine Rees, was a day boy in School House 1902-1910. He was the only son of Dr D Valentine Rees, a much loved Brecon practitioner. An accomplished games player, he gained a blue for rugby football while at Exeter College, Oxford. He also played for the Harlequins and Barbarians and was the president of Brecon Sports Club and Brecon Rugby Club. During the 1st World War he served with the Brecknockshire Battalion of the South Wales Borderers and was seconded to the Machine Gun Corps in 1915.

Before the 2nd World War he hunted regularly and was, for a time, secretary of the Brecon Hunt. His legacy to the school is commemorated by a large stone to the east of the war memorial pavilion. He lived his whole life in the town and maintained a very close association with the school. He was a close friend of my father, Rex.

The next relatively famous figure and benefactor was Lord Brecon, David Vivian Penrose Lewis. He left Monmouth School at 16 and became a diligent Conservative. He was also well known in mid Wales as a keen sportsman, President and Captain of the Crickhowell cricket team and a rugby player with both the Abergavenny and the Crawshays teams. He was a good friend of my father, who played with him, and certainly I remember as a young man being taken in his Rolls Bentley down to watch the Newport team when he was President of Newport.

In the early 1950s the Conservative government created the post of Minister of Welsh Affairs, and Rees served as minister to Henry Brooke the Home Secretary. When he left office in 1964, he joined the board of Powell Dyffryn which has purchased his family quarries; he also became chairman of the Welsh Water Authority from 1973 to his death. He was a man of tremendous energy with a strong sense of public duty, and among his benefactions was the money for a new classroom block at Christ College, Brecon where, thanks to my father's ministrations, he had been made a governor.

Another benefaction took the form of a very generous bequest from G L Alway, a local old Breconian who had followed his father as proprietor of two public houses in the town. George Alway had remained a bachelor and died with no surviving relatives in November 1959. His bequest was of £12,000, a very large sum in those days and the money was used to build a new junior house.

Christ College has not had a reputation for producing large scale entrepreneurs; however, Sir Barrie Stephens, who took over as managing director of a small, barely profitable manufacturing company, Siebe, restructured the company's operations, trimming staff by more than a half, and expanded the company in new directions. At the end of the 1960s he would lead Siebe into the first of what would become a long string of acquisitions. By the end of the decade, while bringing the company's revenues past the two million mark, it hugely increased profits. During the 1970s he transformed Siebe from a small domestic safety products company to a global group targeting the broader engineering controls category. By the end of the decade, Siebe had topped fifty million in sales. Stephens had raised the company's revenues more than a thousand times in thirty years. He was certainly a generous benefactor of his old school Christ College, Brecon.

Other benefactors were (David) Hubert Jones, in particular his widow's gift of over four million to the school for the construction of a science block. He attended from 1917 to 1921. Hubert Jones was a chemist by profession. Also involved in chemicals was Sir Roger Jones of Penn Pharmaceuticals, who has given funds, and Martyn Hazel who gave the money for the Astroturf games pitch. Sir Roger Jones is also a major entrepreneur in Wales, and who chaired the Welsh Development Agency. He has been a governor of the school and showed his affection for it by sending his children there.

Ex-pupil's millions left to top Welsh independent school.

By JENNY REES Western Mail

One of Wales's most prestigious schools has been left a long-forgotten old boy's multi-million- pound fortune to foster a future generation of scientists. As much as 3 million pounds could be left to Christ College, Brecon, after the childless widow of the multi- millionaire decided the school should get his legacy.

The windfall is due to the generosity of the widow of Old Breconian David Hubert Jones, a former science student, who established a successful pharmacy business in Glanaman, Carmarthenshire.

His widow, Florence, who went to live in Llandeilo after his death, died in November 2000. As they had no children, Christ College became a major beneficiary of her will.

The director of the Christ College Foundation, Major General the Rev Morgan Llewellyn, said little was known about the Old Breconian, known as Hubert.

'David Hubert Jones was a pupil here from 1917 to 1921 and was in the school's 1st XI football team and 2nd XI cricket team, but there is nothing else in our school archives,' he said.

What is known is that Mr Jones was born in 1903 and lived in Glanaman. He left Christ College with a certificate in education showing that he had studied Latin, French, history, arithmetic, chemistry and mechanics and from there he went on to study pharmacy in London, where he had two jobs in 1924-25.

He then returned to Glanaman and ran the Central Pharmacy, which is still operating. Yet as Mr Jones died in 1965, there very little is known of him, other than the fact that he was able to pass on 'a very good shop,' as the pharmacy was such a success.

The only surviving relative, Ieuan Jones, who is Florence's cousin's son is also named in the will and lives in Llandeilo.

He said, 'Hubert was very dedicated to his community. Everyone could approach him and he was available at all times of the day.

'He was a founder member of a shooting, hunting and fishing club, Clwb y Mynydd Du.'

He said Hubert's fortune had been accrued from a mixture of family wealth (his father had been part owner of a colliery), business acumen and shrewd financial investment after his death. 'They were of a generation that looked after their money,' he said.

It has taken more than four years for the estate to be settled after there were complications because a children's charity which is now disbanded was intended to get a quarter of the cash.

The school has been left seventy five percent of Mr Jones's widow's residual estate.

'My feeling is that he was a quiet, hard working, successful professional chemist who ran a very good business,' said Major General Morgan Llewellyn, director of the Christ College Foundation, set up to raise money to fund student bursaries and improve the school's facilities.

'He had a quiet family life and didn't have any children, but obviously felt a sense of gratitude to Christ College for presumably teaching him chemistry in the first place.'

'The school was happy to comply with Mr Jones's wishes that the money should benefit chemistry students', he said.

'A shortage of science students is having a major impact not only on the future of medical science in the UK, but also on engineering and the technical industries. These are areas that in the past the UK has taken a lead.'

'We propose to enlist the help of the medical and teaching professions to seek out those students who would most benefit from this wonderful opportunity.'

'This public-spirited legacy might also provide a spur to other potential benefactors to join in a partnership with Christ College, which will further expand and enhance this exciting initiative aimed at promoting the traditional sciences.'

Head teacher Philip Jones said, 'We will not know the exact size of the legacy until later in the year, but it is significant and certainly over six figures. It will enable us to fund up to thirteen bursaries and enhance the school's already excellent science facilities.'

The school has been in existence for 477 years, and boarding students pay £16,800 annually, with day pupils charged £11,250. The school has never had an endowment, so the Foundation was set up in 2001 with an ambitious target of ten million pounds needed for bursaries, along with a similar sum for capital improvements. It is hoped the seven-figure legacy will go some way to redress the national shortage of scientists. Students the length of Britain have shown their love affair with science is on the wane, but this independent school has been bucking the trend over the last nine years and thirty four percent have gone on to read science at university.

In 2003 of nearly 350,000 students starting degree courses, less than one percent pursued the traditional sciences of physics and chemistry. In many areas the limited availability of A Level courses in maths and sciences is also deterring students.

This shortage is having dramatic consequences on physics and chemistry departments with many of them forced to shut down in major universities across the nation; the University of Wales, Swansea is considering closing the chemistry department'.

Another benefactor was W Hugh Phillips, formerly high sheriff of Gwent, who has, among other gifts, given help to the music department. Guy Clarke who was for many years chairman on the finance committee of governors, should also be mentioned here as he has done a very useful job of managing The Old Breconians Charitable Trust.

Also the Thomas family of Garthbrengy have been one of the biggest farming families in the school with 9 pupils attending.

The school would be a very different place without all these benefactors and the contributions of many local parents.

There has been a tremendous link between Christ College and the farming community. Today, people like Vin and Rob Stephens, great rugby players, Margaret, Rob's wife has also done much sterling work in the offices and Terry Stephens and Frank Roderick,the Williams' Greenway, also Brian Jones were at the school; in the past there were people like Elwyn Jones who was High Sheriff and had a famous herd of Hereford cattle. Also, the Thomas family of Garthbrengy have been one of the biggest farming families in the school with 9 pupils attending.

Two families we haven't really mentioned are the De Winton family, who over the years have provided governors including Cathy Bishop and also provided finance for the school; their fortune was based on the Wilkins Bank in Brecon, and the Raikes's family also provided governors including Vice Admiral Sir Iwan Raikes and General Sir Geoffrey Raikes.

A further benefactor has been Martin Hazel of Newport, who had a large-scale haulage business and chaired Newport Dragons, who gave the all weather pitch to Christ College.

So many local families have done so much for Christ College. The school would be a very different place without all these benefactors and the contributions of many local parents.

SIR PAUL SILK

THE POLITICIANS AND THOSE INVOLVED IN POLITICS

There is a theme that runs through these politicians and it is a leaning towards the left. Whether Christ College had anything to do with this is not certain, but as a Welsh public school, an outsider to the English establishment, this could have caused a perception of anti-establishmentarianism among its cleverer and more politically aware pupils. The first man on the edge of politics that we know about was **William George Leonard Hall**, 2nd Viscount of Cynon Valley, son of George Hall, a mineworker who became a Labour party Member of Parliament and cabinet minister. Hall won a scholarship to Christ College, Brecon, but left school to become a miner at the age of 15. He subsequently joined the Merchant Navy but soon re-entered education, receiving medical training at University College Hospital and becoming a member of the Royal College of Surgeons. In 1938 he was appointed Assistant Medical Officer for Merthyr Tydfil. He gave up the post in 1940 during the 2nd World War, becoming a surgeon and commander in the Royal Navy Volunteer Reserve.

In 1946, Hall returned to civilian life as a medical officer for the Powell Dyffryn Group, the coal mining company, quickly moving from a medical position to become a director. He later held a post as Director of Investments for Africa, Asia and the Middle East for the International Finance Corporation. In 1969 he was appointed the first chairman of the Post Office although his tenure was to be short. He had been appointed by John Stonehouse, Post Master General of the Labour government of Harold Wilson, and when the Conservative Party won the general election, he was dismissed from his post, which caused a number of sympathy strikes by postal unions, causing

69

disruption to postal services. He then went on to be an active member of the House of Lords.

Sir Evan Paul Silk was born on 8th February 1952 in Crickhowell, Powys. He went to Christ College, Brecon in the 1960s, and became a great friend of the author. He went on to read Greats at Brasenose College, Oxford and the author remembers many trips to Oxford and reciprocal trips from Paul to RMA Sandhurst where the author was situated. He proved a great friend; when the author came back from Belize having served with the Royal Regiment of Wales as a broken man, and went into the army mental hospital at Woolwich, he will never forget the number of trips Paul made to see him, coming from the other side of London to do so.

Silk was not a politician but served as House of Commons clerk for a total of almost twenty five years, clerking at different times, three departmental Select Committees including the Foreign Affairs and Home Affairs Committees. He was a former Clerk of the Welsh Grand Committee and Clerk in charge of the Government of Wales bill. He also contributed to drafting the first standing orders of the Welsh Assembly. He has written and lectured on Parliament and the Constitution. His father was an eminent headmaster at Blaina Grammar School, having been awarded a mention in *Despatches* in the First World War and was in the same battalion in the Welch regiment as the author's grandfather; they were both adjutants of the regiment sometime during the 1st World War. I may be talking out of turn, but Silk, like the author, was a believer in Wales standing on its own two feet within the structure of the United Kingdom. He is a man of enormous integrity, a great friend to have and it is marvellous that he is chairing, at the present time, the governors of Christ College, Brecon.

Sir Simon Hughes was at Christ College at the same time. He was very progressive in his views at school, and through his influence as head boy, he managed to abolish the beating of junior boys by senior boys, and fagging. After Selwyn College

Cambridge, he was first elected to Parliament in the Bermondsey bye-election in February 1983. It was a notorious campaign against the gay rights campaigner Peter Tachell. What was paradoxical was that Hughes was later outed by *The Sun* newspaper as bisexual.

Hughes eventually lost his seat in 2015 after being an MP for thirty two years. In December 2013 he was appointed as Minister of State for Justice. He stood for the Liberal leader election in 2006 and campaigned under a slogan of 'Freedom, fairness and sustainability'. Eventually he came third in the ballot of party members, behind Campbell and Huhne. Simon was a prominent member of the House of Commons for many years, although he attracted criticism by some people such as Dennis Skinner who felt he preached at MPs.

Roger Williams CBE was the MP for the constituency of Brecon & Radnor from 2001 until he lost his seat in the 2015 general election. He studied at Christ College, Brecon and Selwyn College, Cambridge. On graduation in Natural Sciences, he returned to Breconshire, becoming a livestock farmer at the family farm near Llanfilo. During the mid 1980s he was elected chairman of the Brecon and Radnorshire branch of the National Farmers Union. Williams joined the Labour Party in 1969, but left to join the SDP at the formation of that party in 1981. In 1990 he was elected Chairman of Brecon Beacons National Park.

After the retirement of fellow Liberal Democrat Richard Livesey in 2001 he was elected to represent the constituency of Brecon and Radnor. In 2005 he was returned with an improved majority in the general election and was re-elected in the 2010 election with a majority of 3,747. There is no doubt that in many circles he was a popular MP, having the personal touch, and knowing so many people in the constituency. He was slightly ambivalent about his roots in a public school, but the education at Christ College did him well; he also was a prominent rugby player which gave him even more contacts.

It was a surprise at the end of the coalition government that

Roger Williams wasn't taken into the Lords, but of course the Liberals had a disproportionate number of Lords to MPs and therefore it was very unlikely he would get a position there. The demography of Brecon and Radnor has changed over the years, and with the influx of many people, especially from the English middle class, and with the decline of Nonconformism, the popularity of the Liberal Democrats has declined. Whether they can ever recapture the seat remains to be seen.

The author too, is a Liberal Democrat, as were many of his family; he has a prize picture of Lloyd George addressing an assembly in Llandovery with his grandfather Dr Tom Morgan presiding as chairman of the meeting. There is quite a strand of Liberalism that has run through Christ College through the years, and some of these politicians afore mentioned emphasise this.

Another interesting Old Breconian of note is Geoffrey Hinton who was station commander of the Secret Intelligence Service in Cairo in the late 1940s. Hinton was a friend of Philby's and both had worked together intermittently since 1944 Section V days. As SIS station commander, he'd tell Philby all he wanted to know, probably unwittingly. We know very little about Hinton because, possibly due to security, there is very little information available on him on the internet, and Christ College cannot locate an obituary on him.

DR TEDDY MORGAN

SPORT AT CHRIST COLLEGE BRECON

This is a slightly prejudiced chapter, because it involves my own family, seven of whom were first class rugby players.

Probably the most famous was Dr Teddy Morgan who was born in Rose Cottage, Abernant, the son of William Morgan, a draughtsman in the pit, whose brother Edward Morgan was the agent to the Marquis of Bute in the Aberdare valley. The latter was a single man and it was his money which sent William Morgan's three boys to Christ College, Brecon where they were all outstanding sportsmen. Dr Teddy played for London Welsh and Swansea, and obviously at Guy's Hospital where he trained as a doctor. He played sixteen times for Wales and scored fourteen tries for them; he had about the same number of caps. He scored the famous try in 1905 which beat the All Blacks, although he was convinced that the All Blacks later on scored a try which was disallowed, but he believed, was grounded. He is said to have started the tradition of leading the Welsh team in singing the Welsh National Anthem before the match in response to the All Blacks' Haka. As well as playing for London Welsh, he played for Cardiff and Newport.

He was Vice-Captain of the British Isles team that went to play Australasia in 1904, but the English Captain, Bedell Smith was injured in the first match and Teddy took over as Captain. Later, he went on to be an officer in the Royal Army Medical Corps. He is said to have shot tigers in India when he was attached to the army and generally was a first class shot, who lost the use of an eye later whilst shooting in Norfolk.

Dr Tom Morgan, Teddy's brother, and my grandfather played rugby for Guy's Hospital and Blackheath, and was the GP in Llandovery. He had one of the first cars in Carmarthenshire and was well loved in the community. The third brother, William (Willie) Morgan played for the Barbarians and Cardiff and also the Anglo Welsh team which toured Australia and New Zealand, with his brother Teddy. He had a garage outside Paris and also played for the French team, Stade Bordelaise. He eventually came back to Wales, slightly down on his luck and was met by an old friend Dai Owen in the middle of Aberdare, and when Dai asked him what he was doing, he opened his briefcase and it was full of French letters which he was selling!

Perhaps the most interesting of the Morgan family was Teddy's son Guy Morgan, who went to Haileybury, not Christ College; he then went on to Merton College, Oxford. He became a lieutenant in the Royal Naval Voluntary Reserve during the 2nd World War where he commanded a Corvette in the Atlantic, sailed the ship in to rescue partisans in Yugoslavia, was shot, wounded and taken prisoner. He wrote a famous play called Albert RN about a dummy in a prisoner of war camp, went on to become William Hickey in the Daily Express and finally ended up as Douglas Fairbanks Junior's scriptwriter. His most famous film was Anna Karenina with Vivian Leigh as the star. He was truly international.

Dr Tom's three sons, my father included, referred to elsewhere in this book, also included Guy Morgan who was a great rugby player who had four blues for Cambridge where he was at St Catherine's College and as Captain, was an incredible drain on his father's purse because he had to provide a lot of the entertaining at the Varsity. At the age of 22 he was the captain of Wales, and he'd played about eight games for Wales, four as Captain. He also captained Glamorgan at cricket and went on to become a housemaster at Radley College, where Dennis Silk the warden said he was one of the toughest men he had ever met, as, soon after he went to teach there he developed rheumatoid arthritis and coached rugby and cricket on sticks.

The other brother, Noel, was in the Royal Navy in the war. He disliked the thought of being an officer so stayed as a rating and I've heard was sunk but survived and went on to become the chief cashier of the main National Westminster Bank in Cardiff.

He not only played for Cardiff at rugby and was a Welsh trialist but had a reputation for laziness which sometimes meant that instead of running for the line, he stopped and tried to drop a goal. Jonathan Morgan, Rex's son, was the only member of the family to captain Christ College and on one occasion, to captain Sandhurst.

Nicholas Morgan, the author's brother, captained the seconds for two years and is now a successful trust tax and probate lawyer in Oxford.

Rex's uncle Tommy Williams was a superb sportsman at Christ College but unfortunately played in a low grade side. In the March 1894 edition of the *Old Breconian* he was ranked as one of the very best forwards the school has ever had, a very strong runner and a tackler from whom no one had a chance of escaping. He was very dangerous near the line, a consistent scorer and with all his brilliant open play, no shirker of hard work. A first-rate place kicker, he had a trial for Wales but damaged a retina which also prevented him from being a surgeon.

Jonathan also had an interesting cricketing career, playing a few times for the South Wales Hunts and playing mistakenly for the Emiriti, the old boys of the Roman Catholic schools where he scored fifty for them at Eton against the wine trade, and fifty at the Hurlingham Club with a string quartet playing in the background. The most spectacular match was high up in a coffee plantation in El Salvador for the Royal Regiment of Wales against El Salvador.

The first rugby match against Llandovery College was played in 1865 and was only stopped a couple of years ago as a result of the imbalance between a Brecon side which was so much weaker physically than a Llandovery side that in the last ten years had developed into one of the best school sides in the country, latterly coached by my old Sandhurst friend Iestyn Thomas. The success of the team attracted more and more rugby players to the school at Llandovery, and it almost became a rugby academy with players like George North and Andy Powell playing for the school.

During the 1960s, when I was playing, we lost 6-5 and 6-3 to Llandovery, who were coached by the great Carwyn James. It was an enormous accolade to our coach Don Jackson. The team consisted of a great bunch of guys: John Brinckley (who now runs a successful number of restaurants in London), P C K Rees (who was senior major of the RWF), R A L Davies (a successful banker), Mervyn Fudge (a lawyer), Alun Thomas (the former bishop of Swansea & Brecon, and Jack Thomas's nephew), Chris Hill (now a businessman), Martyn Lewis (with whom we have lost touch), M L John (who unfortunately died early, but worked in the National Health Service), David Bodycombe (whose brothers also went to Christ College and are a well known Swansea family), Hugh Deuxberry (who was a lt Commander in the navy and who died recently), Dave John (who worked for the social services), Hilleth Yendell (who has worked all over the world) and R T Hughes (who had a very successful hotel in Aberdovey).

In later years, some success was achieved by master coaches Mike Francis, John Williams and Chris Webber,who respectively coached the firsts for ten , seventeen and ten years I should mention here Tim Trumper, who has helped in the background, and whom my godson and his parents think is a terrific housemaster.

We must never forget the huge work that went into keeping the grounds pristine and we have a lot to thank our great groundsman Dai Price for, who was there in my time.

It is with huge sadness that many old Llandoverians and Old Breconians saw the demise of the great historic match between the two schools. In 1988, Llandovery College had established 64 wins, Christ College 26 wins and 9 draws. My Uncle Guy said, out of all his matches, Wales against England, Oxford against Cambridge, it was the most nerve racking because you had to live with everyone in the school afterwards. There was a period between 1924 and 1958 when Christ College didn't beat Llandovery, so there has been a precedent for what has happened recently, and maybe, the match will come back.

Five Breconians have captained Wales on a total of twelve

occasions; seventeen Breconians have played for Wales and one for England. Thirty five Llandoverians have played for Wales and six Llandoverians have captained the country. I believe there were five old Breconians, the equivalent of British Lions, who went on tour with the Anglo-Welsh side to New Zealand in 1904. I don't believe any other school has achieved this many players on one tour. Rugby as a game has tremendous potential, as shown by the recent British Lions tour to New Zealand. It builds character and a team spirit which is almost as regimental as the army. The public schools dominated rugby in its early years in Wales, and even today make a substantial contribution.

One of the two most recent Welsh players for Christ College was RA Ackerman who played on the wing for Wales v New Zealand in his first season of senior rugby and also toured NZ with the British and Irish Lions. He also played rugby league, when he represented Wales five times. He went on to teach at Christ College, Christchurch, New Zealand, and coached the 1st XV there in 2008, going on to become director of coaching for rugby at Haileybury College, Melbourne, Australia.

Ackerman attended Christ College Brecon at the same time as Simon Griffin, who captained Oxford University in the victorious 1986 Varsity match. The other most recent player was Andrew Lewis, who played prop for Wales and had the most caps of any player under coach Graham Henry. He became a successful investment broker in Cardiff and is now on the board of governors of Christ College, Brecon and lives just outside the town. The most recently capped player was Keiran Marmion who was capped fifteen times for Ireland and played a marvellous game in the recent Irish win against England.

We must also remember Bryan Richards, who taught at Christ College, had one cap for Wales and went on to be a housemaster at Rugby, and Gary Halpern who played prop for Ireland, scoring against the All Blacks and has done a wonderful job helping to coach Christ College in recent years. We must also wish James Vickery a much capped varsity player, our new and very dedicated coach good luck for the future

Originally, the two main sports at Christ College (as a single sex school) were rugby and cricket. Both were great team games. In my father's words in the Centenary Programme of the Llandovery match, he says, *'In my long and close connection with Christ College as both master and boy, I saw some fine Brecon sides and outstanding players, but year after year we were defeated. Perhaps they were tougher and stronger – certainly they always exploited every advantage, but is this a reason for getting rid of the Match?'*

A huge camaraderie grew up between the boys of both sides over the years and it seems so sad to lose that. Maybe the fixture may again continue – let us hope so.

THE REV G REX MORGAN

REX MORGAN, OLD BOY, PADRE AND CHAPLAIN

Rex was born in Llandovery and his father was an old Breconian, Dr Tom Morgan, who had played rugby for Guys Hospital and Blackheath, and was the GP in Llandovery town. Rex went to school at Christ College, Brecon, and if not possessing the exceptional athletic gifts of his elder brothers, he was a more than useful member of the 1st XV and the 1st X1. He was also a prefect. He left school in 1929, and after a brief career in banking, went to St David's College, Lampeter and was ordained. Meanwhile, he played fly half for Cardiff Rugby Club and was second string wicket keeper for Glamorgan Cricket Club. He was curate of Llanelli, Breconshire and Sketty, where his vicar was Canon Stewart, the author's aunt's father, and his fellow curate was Jack Thomas who later became Bishop of Swansea and Brecon. It is interesting that Canon Stewart's son joined the South Wales Borderers and later, unfortunately, committed suicide. During this time, Rex met Dylan Thomas but had to stop associating with that particular group because inevitably he was wearing his dog collar and Dylan Thomas's bad language and behaviour meant Rex had to stop joining them.

He joined the army as a regular chaplain just before the outbreak of war in 1939 and was attached to the Guards' depot at Pirbright where he was a chaplain with Lt Col Gethin Jones's father who was the grandfather of Davina Hogg, who had two boys at Christ College. He was then appointed chaplain to the King's Royal Rifle Corps and sent to Calais with the regiment. They were ordered to delay the Panzer Divisions bearing down on Dunkirk. Churchill ordered their commander, Brigadier

Nicholson, to hold out to the last man. They were subject to terrible bombardments, in the middle of which Rex was under an arch when a shell took out two soldiers behind him and he got a splinter in his hand. He was said to have given Airey Neave his last rites at the Battle of Calais in 1940 when the latter was badly wounded.

Later, when the prisoners were taken through France, in a letter from Airey Neave, he said how much he'd enjoyed his chats with Rex. In Neave's book, *'The Flames of Calais'* he wrote, 'To Rex Morgan, in memory of his gallant part in the battle.'

After a fairly traumatic trip to Germany from Calais, Rex was imprisoned in a number of camps ranging from the deep south to the far north of the German Empire. As a chaplain, I believe he was not allowed to escape because he was committed to his fellow prisoners, and he was also moved around by the Germans to fill any vacancies in camps. However, he was on an escape committee and he allowed his letters to be encrypted into code despite quite a risk to himself. He also had to deal with many prisoners with mental distress and had a library of books, especially on Jung which he used to help people. On one occasion he was sent to a punishment camp for complaining about the treatment of his fellow prisoners. It was not a hugely restrictive camp, but worse than the ones he'd been used to. It was said by Squadron Leader Room who was in the camps with him, that 'There are two sorts of doctor or chaplain in the services; one is a service chaplain and the other is a chaplain in the services. Unmistakably, your father was a service chaplain and he was remembered with the greatest respect and affection by something like 800 prisoners of war to whom he administered. '

Rex was in Stalag Luft 6 in Lithuania and was in that terrible voyage down the Baltic in an old coal ship when the prisoners were crammed into a hold full of coal dust with only buckets lowered by the guards for the use as latrines. He himself had great difficulty going in and out of the hold because he suffered from vertigo. They were then taken on a terrible five mile run when they were bayoneted and dogs were set on them by the Nazis, although Rex was able to avoid some of this as he was in a cart with the doctor at the back of the run. They were placed in a horrible camp called Stalag Luft 4 at Tychow.

In July 1944, when the Russians were advancing from the east, Hitler was determined that the prisoners should be held as hostages and not captured by the Russians. The camp was reckoned to be the worst prison camp of all and was run by a gang of three madmen, who were ardent Nazis, and who took their orders from the Gestapo. The prisoners had eight ghastly months there. As the Russians advanced, the men set off on the dreaded long march, which became known as the 'Shoe Leather Express March'. According to Room, '700 of us left on Feb 6th, 1945 and only 540 reached the end and were liberated.' Starvation, illness, weakness and disease, notably dysentery and typhoid were rampant, and men fell out of the column every day. Many of them were left to die at the roadside and some of them were even executed by the Germans. They even lost thirty-five of their own comrades when RAF Typhoons bombed the column, thinking they were German troops.

During the day, the prisoners marched four or five abreast and at night were herded into nearby barns. With luck, a bed consisted of straw on a barn floor. Sometimes, however, the Germans withheld clean straw saying the prisoners would contaminate it making it unfit for livestock use.

On one occasion, so many men crowded into a barn that some had to sleep standing up, and if no barn was available, they bivouacked in a field or forest. We should remember that this was at the height of that terrible Polish winter.

Sometimes, food was so scarce that the prisoners ate raw rats. Snow piled knee deep at times and temperatures plunged way below zero. Virtually every Prisoner of War became infected with lice. Dysentery was rampant, and some men drank from the ditches that others had used as latrines. Dysentery made bowel movements frequent, bloody and uncontrollable. Men were often forced to sleep on ground covered with the faeces of those who'd passed before them. Desperate for relief, they chewed on charcoal embers from the evening cooking fires. Some men even welcomed the frequent foodless days because it made the dysentery less severe.

Rex was said by Squadron Leader Room to have performed heroically on the march, helping very many men. Some severely ill prisoners were delivered to hospitals passed en route and usually never seen again, while straggling marchers were sometimes escorted into the woods by guards and executed. From beginning to end, the march spanned eighty six days and an estimated 600 miles. Many survivors went from 150 lbs or so to perhaps 90 and suffered injuries and illnesses that plagued them during their entire lives. The death march across Germany ranks as one of the most outrageous cruelties in the German sector of the war; fittingly, a memorial to these soldiers now stands on the Polish ground where Stalag Luft 4 once stood.

Rex came home emaciated but was told by the army they were sending him to the Far East. He'd had enough, and Archbishop G E Williams offered him a job at Christ College, Brecon as assistant chaplain. There, he coached the 1st XV and the 1st X1. He was a producer of plays and chairman of the games committee. He was a wonderful housemaster of the hostel and married Glenys, who gave him a huge amount of help as a housemaster's wife. After more than twenty years at Christ College he left the school to become firstly vicar of Cathedine, Bwlch and Llansantffraid and later after a heart attack, the vicar of a slightly less demanding parish at Libanus and Llanspyddid. He was an inveterate smoker, and this contributed to his relatively early death at the age of 70, just after he'd retired from the Church.

Rex Morgan was a man who never blew his own trumpet but was one of the great Welsh chaplains of the 2nd World War. His brother's fame on the rugby field eclipsed his own wonderful achievements, which does not say a lot for the sense of perspective that the Welsh public has. Christ College, fittingly, has put up a tribute to his heroics on the march, in the chapel at the place where he preached. He was loved by many generations of pupils and his name will always be remembered.

84

My father could never have achieved as much as he did as a housemaster without the sterling work of my mother Glenys. Her father, Major Tom Morgan had been adjutant of 15th Welch at the beginning of the 1st World War and she had been educated at Edinburgh Ladies' College, although a Welsh girl.

Glenys's mother came from an old Swansea coal-owning family and being the product of sterling genes, she was able to help father enormously. She was supported by a wonderful staff including Ruby Morris and Betty Edwards, and Mrs Brown who ran the most efficient laundry set-up and was the mother of Pam Chappell who is a great friend of the author.

EMMA TAYLOR

STAFF REX AND JONATHAN KNEW

Father was very fond of Canon AD James, the headmaster of Christ College, who was related in some way to my mother. His brother was headmaster of Harrow. When he developed health problems and retired in 1956, the school at the time numbered only 190 pupils. Canon James was a great classicist, as were all the headmasters until the appointment of Dr John Sharp in 1962.

In the 20th century, two men, Canon Donaldson and Geoffrey Isitt both taught in the school for fifty years. In the early 1950s, a considerable proportion of the teachers, five out of the thirteen, were clergymen. Geoffrey Isitt's son David was my brother Nick's godfather and went on to become Chaplain of King's College Cambridge and should have been a bishop but was involved in those early years in the marriage of a divorced clergyman which was not approved of.

In 1956 Mr A D D McCallum came to the school as headmaster. He was a former colonel in the army and was an extremely dynamic man. He brought a Scottish influence to the school and in many ways restored its fortunes. My father Rex was a little wary of him as he found him a bit pushy, but that is what the school needed at the time, and my good friend, Chief Inspector Mike Muir formerly of the Metropolitan Police has told me a number of tales and about the time when 'Jock' McCallum was very kind to him after his father had died, partly of wounds sustained in the war.

Father left when a young headmaster, Dr John Sharp, arrived and my feeling is that he'd had enough of youngsters telling him what to do.

One of father's great friends was my godfather Bob Jones, who in many ways was an outstanding poet and English master. I include his poem:

'Enigma'.

The low fire's sudden flickering
Gleams on her polished finger-nails
And fashionable sapphire ring,
Curled round a book of fairy-tales.

Her dress suggests a mannequin,
Her hair arranged with artful grips,
But wanton flames illumine
A curving innocence of lips.

She reads in a seductive pose,
Tempting an amorous enterprise,
But thoughts inspired by expensive hose
Disperse before her expressive eyes.

Madonna on the mantelpiece,
Could you have ever understood
This miracle, this fleur-de-lys,
Sophisticated maidenhood?

There has been a tradition of great masters of English including Gareth Jones, who was a brilliant teacher and his inspiring teaching of *King Lear* and *Paradise Lost* left me with an enduring love for English literature.

The school, in my time, with regard to the houses and prefect system was very hierarchical. I had three fags as captain of rugby, young lads to run around and help me with the more menial tasks. It was Simon Hughes who eventually stopped the tradition of prefects beating other school boys in true liberal fashion, as I have said before. It was a school which was quite Welsh and macho and tended to elevate games players as heroes. My housemaster, when I was head of Alway, was John Payne. He became a terrific servant of the school as Old Breconian secretary and had a distinguished career as a housemaster at Cheltenham and headmaster of Pierrepont School in Surrey. His wife, Ann was ADD McCallum's secretary and a tremendous support to John and to the headmaster.

In the author's time, there was quite an appreciation of the military, and the three musketeers Don Jackson, Eric Pollard and Q Cavanagh were instrumental in pushing appropriate people towards the armed forces. It was rather paradoxical that I was thrown out of Don Jackson's cadre for being too scruffy when I had just come back having won a scholarship to Sandhurst. Eric Pollard ran a very successful shooting team and I will never forget the wonderful experience I had, having been taken to a small gorge on the river Towy to fish for sewin in the middle of the night by Q.

There was possibly much more cross-fertilisation between the staff and the town in those days. Malcolm Cousins, a lovely man and successful housemaster was very involved with Brecon Little Theatre, David Morgan, who had an excellent mind and a wide range of interests, with his highly musical wife, Christine, was involved in the Brecknock Society and the Friends of the Museum as was Edward Parry, an historian of the school. Also, Kelvin Redford was very well thought of by the Cathedral and its choir as an organist and musician. A fascinating man with experience of living in Paris and all that it pertained to, Colin Kleiser was a tremendous cricketer, who started the famous Cobs cricket X1 which was made up of Christ College Old Boys and staff, and went on for many years, inspiring many cricketers; he was also a jazz pianist, and enjoyed cooking. Alison Hembrow, an extremely well thought-of history teacher, went on to do sterling work in the South Wales Borderers' Museum in Brecon. Richard Slaney with his wife Dorcas has done terrific work with the Brecknock Sinfonia, encouraging tremendous music at the cathedral with four concerts a year. Mike Porter and John Marshall were also very well thought of and long serving scientists at the school.

There were other headmasters, Dr Cook and Mr Hockey whom Jonathan knew little about, but he became a close friend of the next head Philip Jones whose son was in Jonathan's house in Blundells and who became a great fishing companion. As a Welsh headmaster, it was very opportune that he was appointed about the same time as the Welsh Assembly was established.

After Philip Jones, Emma Taylor, the outgoing headmistress, was the first woman to be Head of the school since it was founded in 1541. She has been a moderniser who has brought the school up to date in terms of it being an international and Welsh school. Christ College is not a second class English public school, it is uniquely one of the few Welsh public schools situated in a beautiful national park and should sell itself as such. Emma, in many ways, has been a breath of fresh air with a hugely caring attitude towards the pupils, full of common sense and encouragement. She has been very welcoming to the wider school community such as the Old Breconians and the school has so much to thank her for. Emma leaves behind a flourishing and broad-based outward looking school where so many of the children are extremely motivated and happy.

Rugby and music in particular have been its strengths in the past, but today, with just over half the pupils being girls, the former has not been so successful, but the latter continues to thrive.

Other people to mention are: Simon Spencer and his wife Felicity Kirkpatrick who have served the school so well in their different roles, and have now headed out to Malaysia to promote and initiate Christ College's sister school out there. There are many others, whom I have left out, but I should mention my old friend Lt Col Richard Crockett, now retired, who did so much for the Combined Cadet Force. He oversaw the centenary parade of the CCF and got Brigadier David Bromhead, the great great nephew of Lt Gonville Bromhead VC, of Rorkes Drift fame, to inspect the parade. He has also, with his wife Alison, given invaluable service to Rachel Podger's Brecon Baroque Festival, now firmly established as an important event in Brecon's cultural year, and which also supports and encourages many young local musicians.

Tony and Sian Reeves have done a huge amount to promote

Welshness in the school, and Tony himself has learned Welsh and is a fluent and enthusiastic speaker. Neil Blackburn, the talented and inspiring head of mathematics has done sterling work for which so many pupils are grateful. The dedicated coaches of rugby and cricket in particular, I have mentioned elsewhere. This has indeed been a school full of characters and character, much influenced by its talented staff.

We must not forget the chapel, which has probably had the most influence on Old Breconians throughout the ages. The Chaplain, when Jonathan was there, was Philip David, a cerebral priest of great learning. Many other chaplains had terrific reputations including Major General the Rev Morgan Llewellyn who had been Colonel of the Royal Welch Fusiliers and was a good role model for the boys in particular, a man of some humility, hugely conscientious, and imbued with magnificent leadership qualities. The chapel meant so much to so many.

Felicity would not allow me to leave this chapter without re-emphasising the huge contribution made to the archives by Canon Donaldson, who retrieved what was a very scattered bunch of information and was instrumental in forming the records, from about the 1860s, into some sort of order. So much had been lost before this. We now greet Mr Gareth Pearson as the new headmaster after Emma Taylor; he is a bundle of energy, who is no slouch, having spent nine years in the Royal Marines. He is interested in restoring the rugby to some of its former glory.

Christ College has produced many well-known schoolmasters throughout the British Isles. Not least among these is Joe S Davies, who became master of Haileybury and who steered that school into a successful partnership with Turnford School to make the leap to academy sponsorship.

Haileybury has sentimental value to the author because his father's cousin, Guy, was there, and also his aunt's brother, a Stewart, was there before committing suicide with the S W Borderers in Egypt. Also, his spiritual mentor, the Rev Major General Morgan Llewellyn was there as a boy.

Before signing off this chapter, we must pay tribute to the work done and service given by Jo Robinson-Davies, secretary to a succession of heads, who has done so much to smooth the transition from one head to another.

Others we should not forget in our litany of praise is Pete Abbot, who has served 31 years as maintenance manager and caretaker; we must also remember Derek Jones who served with Pete for 21 years and recently died. P.O.J. Rowlands who was headboy around 1950 and has put huge service into the scouts in Brecon for 50 years; David Bush whose contribution has been even greater thanks to his two year attachment to Estyn, the school inspectorate in Wales, and Neil Blackburn who has also done huge service for the school, both as masters; and Jo Copping and Cathy Morrell have been wonderful in the sanitorium.

We should praise the art department and Paul Edgley in particular, a fantastic teacher of photography. We must also remember Terry and Jackie Heath who gave long service to the school and Councillor Mike Gittins who has been on the board of Governors for at least twenty years.

We should never forget the doctors who have served the school, especially people like Sandy Cavenagh and Dr Arwyn Davies, and of course not forgetting the much loved Dr Ken Price who was an old Breconian and a GP in Brecon for many years.

JONATHAN REX MORGAN

JONATHAN MORGAN

Jonathan Morgan writes:

For the first 13 years of my life I was brought up in Donaldson's House, Christ College, Brecon where my father was housemaster and chaplain. Ironically, for an Anglican clergyman, he sent me to St David's Convent, Brecon from the ages of 3 to 8. This created a foundation based partly on the mystery of the church which has stayed with me for the rest of my life. The convent educated many of the county families' children and so gave an introduction into this sort of society. After the Convent, I was sent to the Beacons School, Teignmouth, Devon which was named after the Beacons by its headmaster Leslie Daunt who had been my father's house tutor at Christ College and who was very fond of Breconshire. It was a huge separation from my parents, and mother, in particular, hated sending me so far away. It was the first time I felt the strangeness of being 'the other', a Welshman in England.

Although there were half-hearted efforts at the school to integrate us, that is, my younger brother and me, and even with references to the Tudors in singing lessons when we sang various Welsh songs, I always felt slightly different. It was an unnatural setting with all boys with their usual obsessions, crushes and love affairs. The return to Wales and Christ College was a further culture shock because I had become quite Anglicised, and most of my contemporaries were quite Welsh. So again, one felt like 'the other'.

Going back to my father, I don't think he ever beat my brother or me, and although he caned generations of Christ College boys, they rarely had a bad word to say about him. He was also extraordinary for a parson because he never forced us

94

to go to church. My only regret is that my parents rarely talked about their families and the great bravery of my father and his cousin Guy. Neither did they speak of my mother's father, Captain T L Morgan in the 1st World War. Too much emphasis was put on rugby and cricket and if I had known about my family's military history I would have had far more confidence when I was in the army. Dad had left Christ College, partly because he didn't want to be there when we were there. At the time, I was not a great academic or intellectual but won a scholarship to the Royal Military Academy, Sandhurst. Before that, leading on from my time in the Convent, there was a definite supernatural atmosphere at the College, heightened by tales of ghostly presences in the chapel, which was enhanced by my father's position as Chaplain. That influence of the supernatural has also stayed with me for the whole of my life. Sandhurst was a culture shock after the quietness and well cared for existence of living in country vicarages.

I played rugby for the Academy and certainly felt the Welsh were welcome there although one acquaintance of mine who came from the 'valleys' was considered a bit 'downmarket'. My only mistake was to board a train on an unmanned station in order to watch Wales play England at rugby in Cardiff and fail to pay for the ticket which resulted in my being de-under-officered at Sandhurst.

In the last summer holidays, I spent six weeks on attachment to the Muscat Regiment in Muscat and Oman at a time when Sultan Qaboos had ousted his father who had been a recluse, and the new Sultan was showing himself to his people. This resulted in huge gatherings which were attended by the Arabs in their white flowing garments, often letting off shotguns into the air with excitement. It was all reminiscent of the film, 'Lawrence of Arabia' and an insight into the Arab culture. On one occasion I was on the last mule train in the mountains around Saiq.

After this, I joined the Royal Regiment of Wales in Germany. I didn't find them very friendly towards the young Welsh officers; in fact I felt there was a culture of 'white' or English officers in the officers' mess'.

There were entertaining moments in Germany, especially the huge field training exercises when we went off in to the countryside for two or three weeks. I was amazed at how inefficient many of our armoured personnel carriers were. Often, we arrived at the top of a slope with many of them broken down. After one of these exercises, the company commander told me and my young sergeant to take the company of about seventy men to the red-light district in Amsterdam to relieve their frustrations. I told the men I would be going to the Concertgebouw to listen to the classical concerts but unbeknown to them after the concert I would then creep down to the red-light area only to hear the sounds of *Sospan Fach* and *Men of Harlech* coming out of the bars. It was an experience which culminated in a near riot outside our hotel called Le Coq, resulting in my company almost having wholesale arrests. But with some diplomacy we diffused the situation.

It was soon the Battalion's turn to go to Ireland in 1972 and what a horrific tour we had. Six killed and twenty six wounded in one of the most troubled areas, the Ardoyne and the nearby Bone, with its old football pitch and some of the Shankill Road thrown in for good measure. There were gun battles night after night; my nerves were totally frayed and it was only thanks to the strong leadership of John Ayres, our company commander, that we stayed intact with relatively high morale. It was a dirty, fearsome and tragic war. I nearly cracked there partly because I was never called upon to patch up wounded soldiers as I hated the sight of blood and so the feeling that I might not be able to cope stayed with me throughout my time in the army.

I went back slightly early from Ireland to do the Platoon Commanders' course at Warminster and thence back to Germany before arriving for two years at the Welsh Brigade depot at Crickhowell. During this time I terrified myself, partly to overcome the fears I had of my nerve failing, by doing the army rock climbing course, although I had vertigo, then completing the army yacht hand course although I was terrified of the sea, and then the army ski course, which I enjoyed, and finally the mountain leader certificate, which I failed, having been ordered to put up an abseil on a small rock face on Cader Idris and then refusing to go down it because I didn't trust my knots, thereby failing the course.

It was at this time that I was taking a fifth A Level in British Government and Politics to try and get army sponsorship to do International Politics at Aberystwyth University which was one of the most popular courses for serving army officers. Meanwhile, my nerve was virtually gone and I went to Cyprus with Major Morgan Llewelyn but had all the symptoms of what we now call post-traumatic stress which were alleviated when I got to Aberystwyth, partly by a beautiful girlfriend. The cloud that hung over me was that I was contracted to do five years as a result of my university emplacement, but my nerve had finally gone.

But I did not welch out and after a couple of summer holidays with the regiment in Berlin guarding Rudolph Hess among other activities, I rejoined the Regiment in Belize. My nerve had gone and I really confirmed some of the failings that the hierarchy have perceived in some Welsh officers. I was placed far away from the main base in San Ignacio. This was broken up by trips to play cricket in El Salvador, Mexico City where I got drunk with my taxi driver who afterwards drove me through the city with a hair raising drive; also the Regiment tried to get me out of my malaise by sending me as liaison officer of the frigate Scylla to New Orleans where my moment of glory was pretending to be the Prince of Wales at 2 o'clock in the morning in the Museum of Voodoo. After a brief excursion into the jungle, I was sent to Bermuda as second in command of the Company and was to deal with the riots after the hanging of the perpetrators of the Governor General's death.

I came back to the UK a wreck, ended up in a mental hospital in Woolwich and I shall never forget Paul Silk (or Sir Paul Silk as he now is) coming to visit me regularly. The army didn't seem to understand what was wrong with me, and I ended up on the streets of London for a short time before finding more suitable accommodation. After working in Harrods where I was Father Christmas and surprising a Welsh boy by speaking Welsh to him, I soon afterwards had a repeat of my condition (which was eventually diagnosed as manic depressive psychosis) when I ran out of the house without my trousers on thinking I was in the middle of a nuclear war. I came back to a mental hospital In Talgarth and had reached my lowest ebb when I was rescued by what was perhaps a further psychotic experience of being taken to communion by Bishop Lucy, the great ghost at Christ College, and being given the Mass by a wonderful presence.

From that time on I began to recover, although I did have another psychotic experience whilst at the Marlborough College summer school when having seen Siegfried Sassoon's name up on the honours board I went into the chapel and believed I was blessed by the effigy of the Virgin Mary. After this I wanted to go to a job where I felt relatively safe and went back into the public school system which I knew well, and Blundells the famous West Country school where I was Head of Economics. It was very friendly to the Welsh and had a Welsh headmaster and director of studies, so I felt very comfortable there for a time and ended up running a rugby side, a cricket side, and a hockey side. I had eighty in the 6th form which I alone was teaching, I ran the CCF for a year, the clay pigeon shooting, the fly fishing and was a house tutor. I 'blew up' and had another psychotic episode when I saw Henry VIII as a ghost in my bedroom and realised then that feeling slightly beleaguered in an ancient English public school, I was exorcising the Tudors.

I had to leave Blundells and after a number of courses was appointed a part time university lecturer at UWIC in Cardiff where I taught International Politics, European Politics, American Politics and Modern Welsh Identity which was a course I constructed myself to give so many of my students from the valleys a great sense of their own depth and culture when faced with the big bad world.

At this time, I was also vice chairman of the European Movement in Wales, on the board of the National Welsh American Foundation, Chair of the Community Council in

Llanfrynach, Chair of the Liberal Democrats in Brecon and Radnor, Chair of L'Arche in Brecon, for whom I raised about £200,000 for a house for people with learning difficulties, and Chair of MIND Brecon. I raised £10,000 for Combat Stress and about £10,000 for various other charities, but also gave another £10,000 to local charities.

As a result of my fundraising for Combat Stress, I was presented to the Prince of Wales in the Tower of London where I happened to tell him that Oliver Cromwell's real name was Oliver Morgan Williams and that he came from a Welsh family, which surprised His Royal Highness as he was not aware of this. Later I caused consternation in some circles by writing to Lady Thatcher suggesting her maiden name 'Roberts' was a Welsh name and enquired about her possible Welsh ancestry. She wrote back saying her family did not originate from Wales but John Campbell in his biography of Margaret Thatcher said it did. This prompted me to ring up the Adjutant of the Welsh Guards the night before her funeral, to question her attachment to her Welsh ancestry, especially as the Welsh Guards were to carry her coffin.

There is a certain element in the English establishment which, despite the Tudors, thinks it's 'downmarket' to be Welsh. I have been one of the lucky veterans who, having suffered from psychiatric problems, have been given an excellent council flat in the town I love most, Brecon, and although a little short of money, I am quite happy. I feel that despite my military experiences and being part of a minority culture, I have won through and hopefully give hope to other veterans who have had similar experiences.

Finally, I have completed three books, selling about 1,000 copies of each. The first, 'Entrepreneurs of Welsh Origin' to show that the Welsh did create great entrepreneurs; secondly, 'The Tragedy of War': essays on the Welsh War Poets, Artists and Writers and those in Welsh Regiments,' partly to add another string to the bow of my regiment the Royal Welsh as one of the most literary and artistic regiments in the army, and thirdly, 'The Welsh Warrior through the Ages,' to show the bravery of the Welsh and their ability to produce great leaders. These books came out of my study of Welsh identity, and in a globalised world, the need to reinforce it. I am a Liberal, partly because I have a deep love of freedom and partly because of Lloyd George, who was a political ally of my grandfather, Dr Tom Morgan, and his drive to make this country a fairer place.

TORI JAMES

TORI JAMES

THE FIRST WELSH WOMAN TO CONQUER MOUNT EVEREST

by Tori James

What do you do when you're faced with an opportunity that excites and scares you in equal measure? Those were my emotions when I discovered that no Welsh woman had ever climbed to the summit of Mount Everest. There had previously been successful ascents by English, Irish & Scottish women, but no Welsh woman had made it to the highest point on earth.

For many people, climbing Everest starts as a childhood dream. I was certainly inspired by adventure stories and survival techniques as a young child but perhaps having grown up in the relatively flat county of Pembrokeshire I never thought about any specific mountaineering aspirations. During the two years that I studied at Christ College (DON 98-00) I loved being surrounded by the iconic flat topped peaks of the Brecon Beacons. I recall hiking to the top of Pen-y-Fan for Ascension Day carrying with me my clarinet ready to play a short hymn at the top with fellow orchestra members.

Music was a huge part of my life at CCB, but I always admired my peers who had done something to represent Wales in sport, either on the rugby and cricket pitches or on the cross-country track. I recall looking at their framed photographs on the wall of the sports hall wondering what it would feel like to win a cap for Wales and perform at a national level. I enjoyed sport at school and I was prepared to train hard but I accepted that I was not displaying as much talent as some of my peers. In my final year at CCB I learned about a youth development charity called British Exploring. It is in fact the longest running youth expedition organisation in the UK. Samantha Dennison (DEW 93? - 00) had just returned from a six week expedition to Kyrgyzstan with British Exploring and I was keen to know more.

Feeling inspired by her experiences in a remote wilderness environment I applied for an expedition to Iceland the following year and was accepted. This was my first taste of subzero temperatures and it included trekking over the Vatnajokull glacier and ice-climbing on its crevasse walls. It was an incredible experience and I was hooked. Three years after this and having completed a degree in Geography at Royal Holloway University I secured my first full time job working for British Exploring, based at the Royal Geographical Society in London. It was a dream first job, working with others who shared a passion for the outdoors and surrounded by the history of global exploration.

Whilst there I was quick to seize other opportunities to step outside my comfort zone and in 2005 I became part of the three-strong Pink Lady PoleCats team. We became the first all-female team to complete the Polar Challenge, a 360 mile race to the Magnetic North Pole. This took my levels of confidence and self-belief to a new level as I had never even considered that this was something I might be capable of doing. I had always been the shortest in my year at school and to look at me you might never have assumed I would be able to survive an endurance activity of this nature.

My team worked with professional sports psychologists and physiologists to prepare for this race and I began to realise that many outdoor challenges demand a skill set that is not just all about being the fastest, strongest or fittest person on paper. It's about about your mental toughness and resilience. And that's when my boyfriend suggested climbing Mount Everest. I checked and double checked the record books to confirm that no other Welsh woman had reached the top. I knew that opportunities like this were rare and so with excitement and apprehension I embarked on an 18 month programme of training and preparation that would hopefully lead me to the foothills of Nepal and higher.

More challenging than the physical preparation however, was raising the funding to get there. I approached hundreds of companies and organisations for financial support. I knew that securing sponsorship wasn't going to be easy, but I had no idea how many times I would receive letters explaining that there would be no support on this occasion (and this was before the economic downturn). Worse than the letters, were individuals actually saying to my face "You'll never do it".

On reflection, dealing with comments like this and a whole host of similarly negative sentiments, required as much energy and determination as climbing the mountain itself. Alongside our efforts to secure the financial backing we required for Everest we focussed on our fitness and technical skills. My team comprised Ben Stephens (my boyfriend at that time), Omar Samra and Greg Maud, who had all met whilst studying for MBAs at London Business School. We had chosen to work with British mountain guide Kenton Cool to be our guide on Everest and it was clear that we needed to prove ourselves at altitude before Kenton was willing to climb with us on Everest.

Our 'warm up' and real test was on the world's sixth highest mountain, Cho Oyu (8,201m / 26,907ft) which like Everest straddles the border between Nepal and Tibet. This was a six week long expedition and our first opportunity to become familiar with the oxygen systems which we would use on Everest. The reduced air pressure and lack of oxygen, even at the advanced base camp (5,700m / 18,700ft), hit me hard, causing serious headaches and photosensitivity. I doubted by body's ability to cope with extreme altitude and I came so close to packing up my bags and heading home. There is such a fine line between safe acclimatisation to the conditions and the dangers of Acute Mountain Sickness (AMS). If symptoms are ignored it can develop into more serious forms which include High Altitude Cerebral Oedema (HACE) and High Altitude Pulmonary Oedema (HAPE) which can turn fatal within hours. I knew that above approximately 5,500m, even without any symptoms of AMS the body begins to break down and deteriorate, so four weeks at this altitude were set to be a real test of endurance. For one of my team mates however the decision to descend the mountain prematurely was made for him. Ben developed an ischaemia in the back of his eye which caused black spots in his vision and fearing permanent damage to his eyesight he went back down to base camp without attempting the summit.

My own summit attempt was also nearly aborted when an unexpected snowfall made the climbing conditions unstable. With only days remaining on our climbing permits we were uncertain whether there would be one last opportunity for us to reach the top. In high altitude mountaineering you have to accept that there are numerous factors beyond your control but fortunately on this occasion and by the narrowest of margins, the snow conditions allowed a small team of us to climb through the night and reach the summit of Cho Oyu in the early hours of the morning. On 2nd October 2006 I became the first Welsh woman to do so. From the summit of Cho Oyu I was literally able to set my sights on the summit of Mount Everest. Knowing that I had been able to climb to 8,201 metres was a huge confidence boost and coupled with mountaineering in Scotland, Tanzania and the French Alps I started to feel as though I was getting closer to my ultimate goal.

The momentum behind the expedition was now building. Friends and family were pledging support and donations, and with an increase in media coverage on BBC & ITV Wales we were finally able to secure a sizeable sum of sponsorship from Investec Asset Management and the Defaqto Group. This made an enormous difference, especially knowing that people out there believed in us, but for me personally there were still financial risks. I had invested all my savings into it and quit my full time job so that I could find the time to train and prepare. I was 25 years old at the time and whilst it was daunting, I couldn't think of a good reason not to do it. For me, it was a risk worth taking.

On 25th March 2007 we left Heathrow for Kathmandu, Nepal. Ironically, I was exhausted. In spite of detailed advanced planning there were still so many last minute jobs to complete but thanks to my sister Olivia (DON 00-02), who stayed up all night with me, we finally ticked everything off the list and made it to the airport. An expedition to the summit of Mount Everest typically takes 2.5 months and a slow and steady acclimatisation period is key to increasing your chances of safely reaching the summit.

As soon as I was trekking towards Everest Base Camp through the spectacular Khumbu Valley I relaxed. We became immersed in Nepalese culture, taking breaks at remote tea houses, drinking the hot, dark Nepalese tea and eating tasty dishes of noodles & dumplings. Once settled into our dome-tents at Base Camp we began to meet other climbers from around the world and what struck me was that all of a sudden, our shared ambitions to reach the summit of Mount Everest were completely 'normal'. Unlike at home when people would look at you as if you were mad, here, the goal to reach the top was as normal as making a weekly trip to the supermarket. However, the reality of climbing Mount Everest is that there is a lot of sitting around, waiting for suitable weather conditions or for your body to acclimatise. In addition, you are required to retrace your footsteps many times, climbing up to the higher camps, but then returning to lower camps to sleep and allow your body to make the necessary physiological changes.

The Khumbu Icefall just above Everest Base Camp poses one of the most challenging parts of the climb through which you will have to negotiate its unstable slopes and traverse deep crevasses at least ten times over the course of the expedition. The icefall is quite simply an unpredictable and uncontrollable mass of ice and snow. It's like a river of ice which is gradually moving its way downhill. These small everyday movements go undetected by the human eye but when conditions tip beyond their natural balance climbers will not only see avalanches tumbling down the slopes but hear and feel them too. During one descent I heard a boom echo through the valley. I had no idea in which direction the danger lay. Even if I knew, there was nowhere to run. I just had to hope that this particular avalanche was not heading in my direction. Thankfully, I was safe, but it was a terrifying reminder that you can only minimise the risks of high altitude environments, never eliminate them.

In addition to the cold, altitude and unpredictable snow slopes that you have to contend with on Everest, I found that the intensity of the sun brought almost as many problems as the sub-zero temperatures. On cloudless days, particularly in the Western Cwm on route to Camp 2 it could reach 30 degrees centigrade and I struggled to keep cool and protect myself from sun-burn and heat exhaustion.

Almost every day without fail I would question my ability to find enough energy for another day's climbing. At night temperatures would plummet to -20 degrees centigrade and one of the hardest parts of the expedition was to extricate myself from my sleeping bag in the morning in order to scrape ice from inside the tent and prepare for the day's climb. This is where your mental approach to the expedition needs to take over from what your body is telling you. Positivity is everything. Understanding how you create positive thoughts and extinguish negative thoughts is key to you getting to the top.

I would routinely listen to my MP3 player at the different camps on the mountain. Sometimes this would help block out the noise of the wind attempting to rip our tent off the mountain and diminish concerns about the precariousness of our situation; sometimes it would enable me to find energy when I didn't think I had anything left. Taking each day at a time was also important, rather than focussing on summit day too early.

Having spent over one month in the Himalayas and just as I felt I was beginning to acclimatise to life above 6000 metres I experienced a bout of Cheyne Stokes breathing whilst asleep at Camp 3 (7,500m). When sleeping at high altitude, your breathing is controlled by the amount of carbon dioxide build-up rather than your need for oxygen. At night, levels of carbon dioxide in the blood can drop very low and this can cause a complete pause in breathing. Only after the body senses a build-up of carbon dioxide do you start breathing again. I realised that this is what had happened when I awoke suddenly, in a panic, gasping for breath and attempting to get out of my sleeping bag for fear of suffocation. Thankfully I only had one experience of this but it sought to remind us of the dangers of the 'death zone' we were about to enter.

The weather conditions dictate most of the climbing schedule on Everest and I was comforted by the fact I was climbing with individuals who had many years' experience of reading the forecasts and timing an ascent to reach the summit when conditions would be favourable. My team were given the target summit date of 17th May 2007. This would involve climbing to each of the camps to which we had already been (Camps 1,2 & 3) then on to the South Col (Camp 4) to make a night-time departure for the top. I was apprehensive about everything that lay above Camp 3 but excited that a 'weather window' was opening up.

This first attempt at the summit was unfortunately cut short when I became unwell at Camp 2, struggling with heat exhaustion, a headache and a bad stomach. I didn't even have the energy to pack my rucksack ready for our climb the following day and was forced to make the difficult decision to return to Base Camp. I wasn't alone, Ben descended with me, but Greg, Omar and Kenton went on and within forty-eight hours had reached the summit. I couldn't wait to welcome them back to base camp.

I had started to recover and was feeling much stronger now, but when Greg and Omar appeared through the mist and darkness into Base Camp it became apparent that the 'death zone' really does have a huge impact on the human body. They looked exhausted and frail, not the tall, muscular men they were before the ascent. They stumbled over the rocky moraine. When they spoke, their voices were hoarse, their lips were burnt and peeling, eyes bloodshot too. They had achieved their dream, but it looked painful and this caused me to question my own ability to reach the top. Could I really do it too?

Within days I was back on the mountain preparing for my own summit attempt and from Camp 3 we used oxygen to climb the iconic features of Everest's south side; the Yellow Band and the Geneva Spur, named by Swiss climbers in 1952. It is a well-known fact that the bodies of climbers who have lost their lives remain on the mountain and I have been asked on numerous occasion "Did you see any bodies?". In short, "no". To reach the summit of the highest mountain in the world demands a positive mindset and I knew that witnessing injury or death on the mountain would not be conducive to developing and maintaining a 'can-do', positive frame of mind. For that reason, I did not look out for the much talked-about remains of climbers and neither did I see them.

My team were however the first on the scene following the death of a Nepalese Sherpa who had fallen to his death from the Lhotse Face and seeing how fragile life is here prompted me to question all the reasons why I was on Everest and whether I wanted to continue. After some time out to consider what had happened, I made the decision to continue.

At 9pm on 23rd May 2007 I made my departure in darkness from the South Col together with my Sherpa Lhakpa Thundu. I could not help but consider the dangers that lay ahead. What if my oxygen system failed, what if the wind speed increased and we became unable to ascend or descend? There is no rescue once you are in the death zone and I was aware of our vulnerability. Ben and Kenton were ahead and we could make out the dancing pools of light on the snow slopes above us from the head torches of other climbers. Thundu and I made good progress up the corniced knife edge ridge, gaining an altitude of approximately 100m each hour. I tried to re-fuel my body, but my water bottle was beginning to freeze and it was difficult to eat on the move with an oxygen mask covering your mouth and nose surrounded by multiple layers of fleece to prevent frost bite on your face.

For most of the ascent I had to work with my own thoughts. There was no conversation, just the occasional 'thumbs up' from Thundu to check I was OK. I was cocooned in a world of my own and I needed to be my own coach, constantly telling myself that I could do it and that I would be OK. At the Balcony, which represented the half-way point to the summit, my toes were freezing. I was struggling to work out whether they were just cold, or numb and I had to work really hard to rotate my ankles and alter my foot placement to ensure that I wasn't developing frost bite.

As the sun rose on the morning of 24th May 2007 my spirits were certainly lifted. I could see what lay ahead although the summit was still out of view. The Hilary Step was the most significant challenge that now lay between us and the summit of Mount Everest. Even though it's not technically demanding it is more of an awkward section which leaves you absolutely gasping for breath, despite the fact that you are already breathing supplemental oxygen.

After approximately ten hours of climbing the summit was in sight and I could make out the colourful prayer flags which adorned the top. As I inched closer to it I began to realise that my dream was about to become a reality and that the commitment made to eighteen months of training and preparation was going to be worth it. Sitting on top of the world was a unique experience and one that I will never ever forget. Initially I was nervous about sitting down in case I had used all my energy in reaching the summit and could not stand again afterwards.

At first I simply admired the view of snow-capped peaks stretching hundreds of miles into the distance with clouds filling the valleys miles below us. It was a panorama like no other, with the curvature of the earth to remind us just how high we were. The temperature was approximately minus 30 degrees centigrade and the noise of the wind made it very difficult to communicate with Lhakpa Thundu Sherpa, Namgyel Sherpa, Anna Shekhdar and Rob Casserley with whom I shared the summit.

The moment wasn't however filled with celebration because for me a successful summit meant getting back down again safely too and that was going to take at least two days to return to Base Camp. In total I spent approximately forty minutes on the summit, capturing the important summit photographs and video footage before making a safe descent. Reaching the summit of Mount Everest was something that I never dreamt I could achieve and it continues to have a huge impact on my life. I truly believe that everyone can achieve more than they think that they can, and I realise more than ever before how outdoor experiences can positively enhance lives. You don't have to reach the summit of the highest peaks but by setting yourself a personal physical challenge in spectacular surroundings you will reward yourself with more than simply a great view.

It's important to realise however that I didn't reach the summit of Mount Everest by solo means and there are literally hundreds of people who helped me to get there, many of whom were staff or alumni of Christ College. I thank you all again for the messages of support, advice about kit and equipment, help with fundraising events and much much more. Whether you are an Old Breconian or current student at Christ College I hope that this provides inspiration for you to aim high, strive for things you think are beyond your reach and make your mark.

Tori James is a motivational speaker, adventurer and consultant. Her ascent of Mount Everest is captured in the BBC Wales television documentary 'On Top of the World' (2008) and her book 'Peak Performance' (2013) provides a personal account of her journey to become the first Welsh woman to reach the summit. Tori lives with her husband Richard Strudwick in Cardiff and at the time of writing was expecting their first child.

www.torijames.com

Family and CCB: Richard James (father) - SHB 63-66 Olivia Dalley (sister) - DON 00-02 Deputy Head of School / Head Girl Jane James (mother) - School Governor 2003 – present

CONCLUSION

Any school is the sum of its pupils and its history. Generations of pupils have come back to Christ College and in particular, they come to see the chapel, which is the centre of the school spiritually. For a small school, Christ College, like so much in Wales has 'batted above its station'. It is one of the oldest schools in Wales, with one of the finest histories and has produced a large number of liberals and classicists through its teaching of humanities. More recently, science has come to the fore with a magnificent bequest of a new science block. It has held its own financially now for many years and we hope it will go from strength to strength. Christ College has produced its own band of heroes, military, spiritual and sporting, who will stay with the school for ever.

It's motto *'Possunt Quia Posse Videntur'* comes from Virgil's *Aeneid*. The Rev D L Lloyd, headmaster 1879-1890 was instrumental in introducing the motto, and The Breconian was begun in 1884. Lloyd left a flourishing school to become Bishop of Bangor. The motto refers to the rowers lying second in the race who are striving to overtake the leaders; their chances of success are good. It could be translated as, 'They could do it because they believe that they could'. It is a principle which has served many Breconians well in the classroom, on the games field and in their lives beyond the school.

This book is a celebration of its history and especially, it's famous figures. We must never forget the school changed dramatically in 1987, with the admittance of the first girl, Sally Stewart, and also had its first female head recently, in Emma Taylor. Times have changed; the school has moved on and we have a new head, Gareth Pearson, who, having had a spell in the Royal Marines and much experience in famous schools, believes firmly in encouraging character and integrity.

Lightning Source UK Ltd.
Milton Keynes UK
UKHW02f0729200918
329210UK00005B/552/P